ALL RIGHT
Original Wc

Cover art by Janson Straub.

Broken Fences
© Steven Simoncic
Trade Edition, 2017
ISBN 978-1-63092-102-6

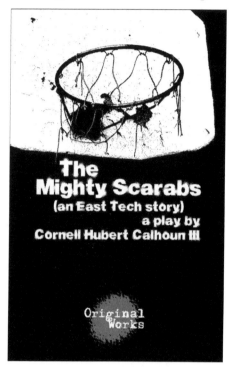

The Mighty Scarabs
by Cornell Hubert Calhoun III

Synopsis: The ball stops bouncing for everyone... eventually. When the heroes of Cleveland's East Technical High School basketball team won the state championship in '55 the world was theirs for the taking. Thirteen years later, the ball has stopped bouncing and reality has set in. A funny, lyrical and mournful exploration of what happens to inner-city hardwood stars when the glory days are a distant memory.

Cast Size: 5 Males, 4 Females

BROKEN FENCES
by Steven Simoncic

Broken Fences premiered May 3, 2013 in New York City, produced by Ballybeg Theatre. The production was directed by Alex Levy.

The cast and crew was as follows:

Hoody:	Clinton Lowe
D:	Erika Rose
Marz:	Emilio Aquino
Czar:	Brian Carter
April:	Krissy Shields
Barb:	Lori Funk
Spence:	Scott Aiello
Esto:	Benjamin Foronda

Costume Designer: Valérie Thérèse Bart
Sound Designer: Howard Fredrics
Lighting Designer: Adam H. Greene,
Set Designer: Kathryn Kawecki
Stage Manager: Allyson Namishia

Synopsis:

In a neighborhood on Chicago's deep West Side, the momentum of gentrification has taken hold and things have begun to change forever. As property taxes rise and demographics shift, Hoody and D struggle to keep the only home they have ever known. But when April and Czar -- a white couple intent on starting a family -- buy their first home and move in next door, the very definition of home is called into question. With unflinching honesty and unapologetic humor, Broken Fences attempts to examine identity and invisibility, community and security, hope and hostility in a modern American urban village that is at once foreign, and the place that these people call home.

Character Breakdown

Hoody: African American male. Early thirties. Engaged to D.

D: African-American female. Late twenties.

Czar: Mid-thirties, Caucasian male. Married to April.

April: Mid-thirties, Caucasian female.

Spence: Late thirties, Caucasian male. Married to Barb.

Barb: Late thirties/early forties, Caucasian female.

Marz: Mid-twenties, African-American male.

Esto: Mid-twenties, Caucasian male who grew up in an African-American neighborhood.

BROKEN FENCES

ACT I / SCENE 1: WELCOME TO THE HOOD

(Lights up on two small urban yards separated by a chain-link fence. The yard stage left is lived-in but well maintained with a small grill, a few lawn chairs, and a weathered picnic table. In the yard stage right, we see April and Czar surrounded by moving boxes. Czar is at the back door of the house. He pulls out a set of keys, opens the door, and sort of presents the house to April. They share a moment of "here we go." She picks up a small box and walks toward the door to enter the house.)

CZAR: Wait. Hold on.

APRIL: What. *(April pauses. There is a beat.)* You're not serious. Czar, this is --

CZAR: Ridiculous, yes I know. But I still think we need to do it.

APRIL: We've been married five years.

CZAR: We've never owned a home.

APRIL: We just sold a condo.

CZAR: Condos don't count. This is a home. We have a house! So, c'mon -- hike it up here.

APRIL: I'm not hiking anything.

CZAR: C'mon, I'm supposed to carry you over the -- it's like a thing you do.

APRIL: If you're a Viking.

CZAR: It symbolizes good fortune.

6

APRIL: It symbolizes taking the wife's virginity, against her will, the night of her wedding.

CZAR: Really? How do you know that?

APRIL: How do you not know that?

CZAR: Because I'm not a Viking.

APRIL: And I'm not a virgin, so...

(Czar's cell phone rings.)

CZAR: (*Answering the phone*) Hey man.

APRIL: Who is it?

CZAR: (*Into the phone*) Yeah -- no, we're good -- so far we've established that I'm not a Viking and April's not a Virgin but we haven't unpacked a thing. What, Seriously?

APRIL: Spence?

CZAR: That's great, but you guys don't have to --

APRIL: Tell him no.

CZAR: Well, yeah, sure -- no that's fine --

APRIL: It's not fine --

CZAR: (*To April*) They're our best friends.

APRIL: He's your best friend.

CZAR: (*Back to the phone*) Okay, but are you sure 'cause -- really?

APRIL: They do this all the time --

CZAR: No that's great -- if you're already -- yep -- we're out back. Yeah, just park on the street. No, it'll be fine. I know, but -- (*To April*) It'll be fine right? Parking on the -- (*off April's reaction he goes back to the phone*) It'll be fine. Okay, see you in a few. (*He hangs up.*)

APRIL: They're coming over.

CZAR: They have Thai food.

APRIL: But they don't have an invite.

CZAR: Maybe they were just in the neighborhood.

APRIL: That's not funny.

CZAR: We could use some food -- the book says you're supposed to eat like every three hours -

APRIL: He's worried about his car isn't he?

CZAR: No, he just wasn't sure if he should park on the street.

APRIL: Which is code for --

CZAR: He's worried about his car.

APRIL: Why?

CZAR: I don't know -- 'cause he watches the news.

APRIL: What's that supposed to mean.

CZAR: It means we're probably gonna get a lot of this.

APRIL: A lot of what.

CZAR: Code. Our friends are gonna be polite and...confused... and concerned about their cars.

APRIL: That's ridiculous.

CZAR: It's also true. Wait 'til your folks visit, they're gonna be speaking Klingon.

APRIL: I don't care -- they're gonna have to get used to the fact that we live in East Garfield Park --

CZAR: And they will. Eventually. But in the mean time, we're gonna have to get used to the fact that when people say things like this place is really neat... it means they think we're fucking crazy.

APRIL: And when they call us adventurous?

CZAR: It means they think we're fucking crazy.

(Spence and Barb enter the yard carrying bags of Thai take out.)

SPENCE: Hey guys -- I think we found it --

CZAR: Spence! C'mon back.

APRIL: Hey guys!

SPENCE: This place is huge, man.

BARB: Wow congratulations -- it's really pretty April.

APRIL: Someday we'll actually figure out where half our stuff is.

BARB: Oh my god we are still missing stuff and we moved like five years ago.

SPENCE: And the car will be --

CZAR: Fine. It'll be fine.

BARB: (*To April*) How are you feeling by the way?

APRIL: Oh you know... Gassy... bloated... have to pee every ten minutes.

SPENCE: You just described my life. I think I'm pregnant.

BARB: (*To April*) Just don't lift anything heavy.

SPENCE: That's what Czar's for.

CZAR: Thought that's why you're here.

SPENCE: I'm here to snoop. Mock you. Eat Pad Thai and drink a really good bottle of white.

BARB: (*To April*) Are you okay with Thai -- we can get something else --

APRIL: No that's fine --

BARB: When I was pregnant my taste totally changed.

APRIL: So far I'm just constantly hungry --

CZAR: I actually think I know where some dishes are.

(*Czar opens a box. He and April begin to pull out a few plates. Spence and Barb open the take-out bag.*)

SPENCE: So... how's it going?

APRIL/CZAR: Good./ (*Overlapping April*) Good so far.

CZAR (CONT'D): I think we're still getting used to the fact that we actually have a house and new neighborhood and all... it's good.

SPENCE: Can I ask you something?

10

CZAR: Probably not.

SPENCE: Was this pure economics or are you like doing a thing here.

CZAR/APRIL: (*Simultaneously*) We're doing a thing./Pure Economics.

CZAR: In addition to the pure economics, I think we thought it'd be good to actually try and find a real, diverse community in Chicago -- with the kid coming we wanted him to grow up in a place where people didn't all look --

BARB: It's a boy?

CZAR: What? No, I just said him because -- I dunno why -- is that dickish?

SPENCE: It's kinda dickish.

CZAR: I don't think it's dickish.

SPENCE: That's probably what makes it dickish. What you meant to say is that you're excited to meet your baby, and boy or girl, you just hope it will be half as beautiful as your wife.

CZAR: (*To Barb*) Does that work?

BARB: It did 'til now.

CZAR: Okay -- we just didn't want our sexless, almost-as-beautiful-as-my-wife child to grow up in a place where everyone looks exactly the same.

SPENCE: Yeah, we didn't have that problem.

CZAR: We looked at all the fashionably gentrifying neighborhoods --

SPENCE: Pricey right?

CZAR: Couldn't touch a house in Logan Square or Ukrainian Village.

APRIL: It was this or going out to the suburbs.

BARB: Well I have to say, this place is really neat.

APRIL: Barb -- when you say this place is neat, does that mean you think we're fucking crazy?

BARB: No... I think it means I think it's neat.

APRIL: See Czar.

CZAR: Spence?

SPENCE: I think you're fucking crazy. But in the best possible way. This is brilliant -- this neighborhood's gonna blow up by the time you flip this.

CZAR: We're not flippers -- we don't flip.

SPENCE: C'mon man. Did you see all the developer signs out there?

CZAR: April wouldn't even let me carry her over the threshold because it's culturally insensitive to Vikings. You think she's gonna let us flip a house?

SPENCE: You remember Creepy Geoffrey?

CZAR: Copywriter?

SPENCE: With the hair plugs... smelled like yoga.

CZAR: He was a hack.

SPENCE: That's why he's in real estate now. He's all over this neighborhood.

CZAR: Well good for Geoffrey but we still need to --

SPENCE: Nail the Tic Tac thing. Yeah, I already did that.

CZAR: Really.

SPENCE: You were out. Wanna know what it is?

CZAR: Not the dirty mint thing.

SPENCE: Fresh mints for dirty mouths. Think of all the dirty things people do with their mouths -- you need a mint.

CZAR: No it's --

SPENCE: Kent loved it.

CZAR: Kent's an idiot.

SPENCE: He's also your boss.

BARB: Are dirty mints a good thing?

SPENCE: It's dirty mouths -- you're not in the target audience Barb. We're going after young people.

CZAR: He means younger people.

SPENCE: Millennials, club kids... Tic-Tacs are gonna be cool again.

APRIL: Were they cool before?

SPENCE: Number one mint in the sixties.

CZAR: They were the only mint in the sixties.

13

SPENCE: Wrong. Mentos. 1948. Read the fuckin' brief. (*Hands Czar a file and a product sample.*)

CZAR: What's this?

SPENCE: Gift from Kent. It's your worst nightmare.

CZAR: We're not working on this.

SPENCE: I don't think we have a choice.

APRIL: What's a Cheese Chunker?

SPENCE: It's... cheese.

CZAR: Product. It's cheese prod - they can't legally call it cheese.

SPENCE: Yeah, well either way, it's the next six weeks of our lives. (*Off Czar's reaction...*) Look, we don't hop on this - they'll give it to two kids straight out of art school that make half as much as we do.

CZAR: Great -- let 'em go nuts.

SPENCE: Yeah but no. See I have a McMansion with a McMortgage and a monthly bill from Waldorf so my child can learn to play with yarn instead of read -- so I'm Cheese Chunking. That make any sense to you?

CZAR: Sort of.

SPENCE: Well now that you're sort of locked into a sort of huge-ass mortgage yourself, you'll sort of realize your nuts are sort of in a vice for the next 30 years, and you'll sort of become a fan of Cheese Chunkers. No offense April, it's a beautiful home.

(*Spence gets up and walks to the fence.*)

14

CZAR: Why is he limping? Why are you limping?

SPENCE/BARB: I pulled a muscle./He got snipped.

SPENCE: I pulled a muscle after I got snipped.

CZAR: I didn't know you got snipped.

SPENCE: No one does unless they talk to Barb for thirty seconds. In case you're wondering, I don't feel like any less of a man.

CZAR: That's not what I'm wondering.

BARB: A bunch of the dad's all went together.

SPENCE: Jesus Barb, enough.

APRIL: You all went together? Like a little club or something?

SPENCE: It's not a club. It's a loose organization of like-minded individuals.

APRIL: Like a club.

SPENCE: It's not like we're all laying spread eagle on the same table or anything.

CZAR: Did that come up?

SPENCE: Getting snipped is what guys in Schaumberg do. They make a whole thing out of it. You grill some steaks, make a pitcher of Manhattans, then you go --

CZAR: Get sterilized with your neighbors.

SPENCE: See this is why I don't tell you things. You'll see man -- your head changes when you have kids.

CZAR: I'm just saying I think it's neat.

15

(*Esto enters the yard next door. We hear tinny/compressed music coming from a blaring pair of headphones on his ears. He doesn't even notice his new neighbors. He is carrying a box that looks exactly like the boxes April and Czar are unpacking. He sets the box on the picnic table, cracks it open, and pulls out some dishes, oblivious to the stare of the people across the fence.*)

SPENCE: What's he doing?

CZAR: I think he's stealing our dishes.

(*Esto begins to unpack more dishes from the box.*)

CZAR: Hey. Excuse me.

(*No response. Esto bobs to the music in his headphones.*)

SPENCE: Hey buddy, we're talking to you!

BARB: Spence!

SPENCE: What!

BARB: You're not supposed to confront him like that.

SPENCE: What are you supposed to do?

CZAR: Call the cops.

SPENCE: For dishes. In this neighborhood.

CZAR: Yes. For dishes in this neighborhood.

BARB: He looks like he lives there.

SPENCE: You don't wanna be that guy man. The cops get to go home - you're already there. So's he.

APRIL: Okay, everybody. Just relax. Excuse me - Hello! I know you can hear me.

CZAR: If you don't turn around we're gonna call the police.

(*This gets Esto's attention. He pauses as if he just heard something, pulls off his headphones, turns around and sees Czar, Spence, April and Barb standing against the fence.*)

ESTO: Sup.

APRIL: Hi. Um... this is really... I think those might be ours.

ESTO: Huh?

CZAR: The dishes. They - look like ours.

ESTO: They do look like yours.

CZAR: Yes. They do, so...

ESTO: What. You think I stole 'em?

CZAR: No. I dunno. I mean it looks like - you sort of have our dishes.

APRIL: Listen, we don't want to make a big thing out of this.

ESTO: Then don't.

CZAR: Excuse me?

(*Hoody and D enter their yard from the back of Hoody's house. They are carrying bags of groceries.*)

HOODY: (*On Phone*) Yo, man. You see Yummy, you tell him he owe me $200. I'm callin' everything in. (*To Esto.*) Thought you was out looking for a job.

(*Esto nods his head toward the other yard. Hoody and D look across the fence and see Czar, Spence, April and Barb. There is a beat as they look at each other for the first time.*)

HOODY (CONT'D): Sup y'all.

(*April, Czar, Spence, and Barb wave/nod and say "Hi." There is another beat.*)

HOODY (CONT'D): Y'all... Need directions or something?

APRIL: Actually, we live here. As of today anyway.

D: Y'all the ones moving in here?

CZAR: Yeah, that's us.

D: Huh.

APRIL: Well, we are. I'm April and this is my husband, Czar. These are our friends, Spence and Barb. (*Spence and Barb say hi/smile/wave.*)

HOODY: All right then -- welcome to the neighborhood. I'm Courtney. This my fiancé D, see y'all already met Esto.

SPENCE: Sort of.

D: Hold on y'all -- I gotta do something --

HOODY: You serious?

D: Talk Hoody. I'll be right back.

(*D runs into her house. There is an awkward beat of silence over the fence.*)

HOODY: So y'all... unpacking and shit.

(*A beat as they all smile and nod.*)

CZAR: Yeah. Dishes mostly.

HOODY: Dishes is good.

CZAR: Yeah -- we love our dishes.

SPENCE: Everybody does.

(*D enters carrying a small square of fabric.*)

D: Here we go y'all -- this for you. (*She hands April the small piece of cloth.*)

APRIL: Thanks. This is great.

CZAR: Wow. That's -- (*Looking at the fabric*) yeah. Thank you.

HOODY: Y'all have no idea what the hell that is do you? (*Off their reaction...*) It's a swatch.

BARB: Like from a quilt.

D: This a little Garfield Park tradition.

HOODY: Started when everyone on this block was related.

D: Whenever somebody from the hood start a new adventure -- good or bad -- they get a swatch.

HOODY: Make a baby -- get a swatch. Somebody dies -- get a swatch. (*Glancing at Esto*) Get out the joint - get a swatch. It's some crazy-ass old school Mississippi shit, but all the aunties still do it anyway.

D: It ain't crazy -- it's for real Hoody. Swatch tells you you ain't alone in the world. Tells you you got some work to do. And then one day when you got a quilt all made --

HOODY: You give a swatch to somebody else who needs it.

D: That's right. You can't stop the swatch -- it just keeps goin' so --

APRIL: Are you sure, 'cause... I don't want to --

D: This ain't me baby, this tradition.

APRIL: Well thank you. Really. Now I'm gonna have to learn how to knit. You don't knit a quilt, do you? Sew. I'll learn how to sew.

D: Good -- you can teach me -- Hoody's momma ain't never forgive me for my sloppy stitches.

CZAR: So this is your place?

(*Hoody nods.*)

APRIL: It's great. How long have you lived here?

HOODY: Whole life. This was my grandma's house, then my mom's and then she left it to me.

ESTO: And Marz.

D: His whole family used to live up in here.

HOODY: Cousins, half brothers, half sisters. Somebody get out the joint, they come here. (*Looking at Esto*) Get kicked out they house - they come here. Half of 'em ain't even related to me.

APRIL: Our family's all over the place.

D: (*To April*) So, it's just the two of y'all in all that house?

APRIL: Actually, we have one on the way.

D: I knew it. I could tell.

APRIL: Really?

D: See how shiny your hair is? When it gets thick like that, that's a sign you making a baby. I knew as soon as I saw you.

APRIL: It just came in -- I never had hair like this before.

D: Every white girl look like Mary J. Blige for 'bout two months when she pregnant.

HOODY: D cuts hair. She a stylist.

D: Training to be a stylist.

HOODY: She good too.

APRIL: That is so cool. Now how about you guys, any babies running around?

D: We gonna start a family soon as I finish school, right Baby?

HOODY: We already got kids (*gesturing to Esto*), you lookin' at one of them.

BARB: We have Tyler. He's 3. (*Showing a photo on her phone.*)

D: So y'all gotta be getting ready for number two.

BARB: Actually Spence just got --

SPENCE: We're good -- we like having one child.

D: (*To April*) Well if y'all need a crib or anything - his momma kept everything.

APRIL: That'd be great -- our family doesn't really do the hand -me-down thing.

D: For real?

HOODY: See my momma's side alone we got 24 cousins. Can't open a drawer around here without a couple cousins flying out. Same pair of pants hits five, six asses before it gets retired.

CZAR: Yeah, we pretty much just have the stuff we brought. Just the stuff in these brown cardboard boxes... these brown cardboard boxes here in our yard.

(Czar is looking straight at the brown cardboard box Esto has on the picnic table in Hoody's yard... Hoody notices the box... followed by D. They both look at Esto.)

HOODY: What -- you helping out Lover Boy?

ESTO: Yeah, man. I was just telling them how I found some of their stuff that was stole.

HOODY: For real.

ESTO: Straight up.

HOODY: See that's good that you found it, 'cause these seem like nice people.

ESTO: Yeah, they seem real nice.

HOODY: And ain't nothin' worse than getting your shit stole the day you move in.

D: That's right. And she pregnant too - she don't need that kind of stress.

HOODY: Personally, I'd like to see the dude that did it get nailed. Specially if he had some priors and what not from back in the day - shit could get weird real fast.

ESTO: Yeah, see they left their truck wide open.

APRIL: That's true, we did.

ESTO: Couple shorties been lifting 'em all day. I figured since you're Hoody's new neighbors, I'd hook you up and get your stuff back.

HOODY: So you like Neighborhood Watch.

ESTO: Just my way of giving back.

HOODY: Another way to give back would be to... just (*gesturing to the box*) give it back.

ESTO: Yeah, right - I was just going through it to make sure it was all there. (*Esto hands the box back over the fence to Czar.*) So, here you go, now we got it all straight and everything's cool. It's cool right?

HOODY: Up to y'all. You may still wanna file a report just to be safe.

(*Hoody holds out his cell phone across the fence.*)

APRIL: No. It's cool.

CZAR: It's cool?

APRIL: Uh huh.

CZAR: (*To Hoody/Esto*) It's cool.

(*Lights hard cut to black. A spotlight fades up on Hoody who is now wearing a black hooded sweatshirt pulled up over his head. As he delivers his monologue, D enters his light and slowly takes the hooded sweatshirt off his back and changes him into a button down Jiffy Lube work shirt. By the end of the monologue, she completes the transformation by handing him a junior college economics text book.*)

23

ACT I / SCENE 2: INVISIBLE

HOODY: I am invisible. Been invisible all my life. When I was a kid I could go days, weeks without being seen. Throw my hood up over my head, eyes pushed way back deep inside, and poof just disappear. Blend into the street another shadow another shade of black and grey on the stairs by the train. Ain't nobody know my real name and that was fine with me 'cause I didn't need one. And I got used to it too, being invisible. I could flow like air, life blowing through me like a breeze. Like I wasn't there. And it was tight too 'cause when you young and you angry and you invisible, you can fuck with people and they don't even know what hit 'em. Can't catch what you can't see. And for a long time ain't nobody see me... 'til one day this light skinned boy from Pilsen pulls out his nine mil acting all gangsta and shit and - POP! POP! Busts two caps just like that. I musta been real invisible that day 'cause that boy from Pilsen never even saw me. Bullet passed through me like a pit bull, clawing and scratching and biting its way out. Woke up in Cook County Hospital with a red Bulls jersey that used to be white packed into my chest. Don't even know how it got there. That was the day I became a little more in focus.

(The lights come up a bit so we get a better look at his face.)

HOODY (CONT'D): After a while I realized the scars weren't just on me, they were me. And every year, I got more. Earned every cut, every burn, every bruise, and every tattoo the more marked up I got, the more I could be seen. At least here in Garfield Park you ain't had to look hard to see me -- I was everywhere, man -- just connect my dots *(Pointing to scars on his arm)* and you got me. Least the old me. The fuck you me. The used-to-be me. Now my shit's retired like Jordan. Ham sandwiches and double shifts, that's all I'm pulling these days. Shit I go to Costco. And I like it. Scars are fading... dots are disappearing... trade your bruise and tattoo for some comfortable shoes... and you're left with a whole lot less to connect.

(The lights fade to black.)

ACT I / SCENE 3: YUMMY IS A PIMP

(A light fades up on Hoody's yard. D is pacing with a book bag, a dented mannequin head and a full head of steam. Hoody enters.)

HOODY: 'Sup baby.

D: *(Gesturing with the dented hair styling mannequin.)* Somebody sat on my head.

HOODY: Who?

D: Some guy nodded out on the Red Line. I gotta dye and style test tomorrow - I got to practice tonight.

HOODY: So get another head.

D: Where am I gonna get another head at seven thirty?

HOODY: You got skills baby, you don't need no practice -

D: Aw, hell no. Don't even start, Hoody. This is Mario Traccocci. They weeding students out every week. They looking for a reason. *(A beat.)*

HOODY: What.

D: Let me use your head.

HOODY: My head? No, no, no.

D: Hoody.

HOODY: Hell no.

D: You gonna be sitting here anyway -- you ain't even gonna notice – *(He gestures. She stops.)*

25

HOODY: I have spoken on this topic. And... you just gonna have to get another head 'cause...

D: Sit down.

HOODY: Damn, D -

D: Sit.

(*There is a brief standoff then Hoody sits. D puts a flowery smock around his neck and begins to lay out her scissors, razor, and hair dye.*)

D: So, how was your day, sir?

HOODY: The hell you mean how was my day?

D: We supposed to develop a rapport with our clients. They grade us on it. So how was your day?

HOODY: Good until now.

(*Just as D gets ready to apply the color, Esto enters carrying a stack of mail and a massive coffee drink with whip cream from Starbucks.*)

ESTO: Aw, hell no.

HOODY: Don't even.

ESTO: So D, we just blowing him out or we getting real with this shit?

D: We getting real with this shit. Highlights. We gonna be a while.

HOODY: How long's a while?

D: Don't turn your head.

(D straightens Hoody's head. She begins to do her prep work. Esto watches, taking a big sip of his coffee drink.)

HOODY: The hell is that.

ESTO: This here is a venti, extra foamy, triple shot skinny soy machiatto with whip.

HOODY: That good?

ESTO: Fuckin' delicious man. Y'all should go up there.

D: Where.

ESTO: New Starbucks up on Kostner.

HOODY: The fuck they put a Starbucks on Kostner?

ESTO: Old Currency Exchange. Got a fuckin' Panda Express going up next door too.

HOODY: How you buying five dollar coffee, man?

ESTO: They givin' 'em out free. It's the grand opening. Your brother's working up there.

HOODY: Marz working at Starbucks.

ESTO: You oughta call him, Hoody. He told me to tell y'all they hiring. I been chillin' up there all day. They got these big ass couches. Footrests and shit.

HOODY: How many of them you drink?

ESTO: Six.

(They all bust up/react.)

ESTO (CONT'D): I'm freaking out man.

27

(Esto polishes off his coffee drink and tosses the cup in the trash.)

ESTO (CONT'D): Yo, I grabbed your mail. Y'all got a bunch more of them letters from the Assessor's Office.

(Esto tosses a stack of letters on Hoody's lap.)

D: We got more letters?

(Esto makes his way upstage to the fridge.)

ESTO: *(To Hoody)* Yo, Beyonce - you want a beer?

D: What are all these letters for?

HOODY: They ain't for nothin'.

ESTO: *(To Hoody from the fridge.)* Yo, Rhianna you thirsty?

D: *(Still looking at the letters.)* If they ain't nothing then let me see.

HOODY: D –

(D grabs a letter out of Hoody's hand. He tries to grab it back but it's too late.)

D: You said you were gonna take care of this.

HOODY: I got some bullshit letters a while ago, but they ain't nobody down there you can talk to so I -

D: Stopped opening the mail. Damn, Hoody, I told you --

HOODY: What's it say?

D: Says we owe $5,278. That's like double last year's. They can't just up and do that.

HOODY: They did it. Currency Exchange becomes a Starbucks, condos going up in the park... We livin' in the lap of luxury now so we got to pay.

ESTO: So don't pay it.

HOODY: Don't pay it, they take your house.

D: Oh hell no, they ain't taking this house! This your momma's house. This your grandmama's house.

HOODY: They ain't takin' my house. I'll figure somethin' out.

D: Well you doin' a great job so far.

ESTO: (*Looking over D's shoulder at the letter.*) 60 days. Fuck, man.

HOODY: Where it say that --

D: Can we get an extension?

HOODY: Not another one.

D: You already got an extension? (*A beat.*) When were you gonna tell me?

HOODY: When I figured out how to pay it.

(*Marz enters with a tray of three large Starbucks drinks.*)

MARZ: Sup y'all.

HOODY: You just lettin' yourself in now? This ain't your house.

MARZ: Technically it's half mine -- she was my momma too. I brought these for y'all. This here's Green Tea Frappuccino, shit's like nine dollars a glass so drink it slow 'cause this ain't no Shamrock Shake and shit.

ESTO: I still can't believe you working at Starbucks, man.

MARZ: This just part of my gig Lover Boy -- I got multiple revenue streams. Economic tide lifting all boats in this 'hood -- better get your dingy in the water man.

ESTO: Okay I have no idea what that means.

HOODY: Means he has two damn jobs.

MARZ: That's right I'm teaching too.

ESTO: The hell you gonna teach?

MARZ: Boot camp.

ESTO: Boot camp class.

(*Marz smiles.*)

ESTO (CONT'D): You mean people pay you money to beat on they ass like they was in the Army?

MARZ: Every goddamn Saturday.

ESTO: Who the fuck would do that?

MARZ: White people. Sixteen of the motherfuckers. Looking for a challenge and shit.

ESTO: How the hell you get hooked up with that?

MARZ: LuLu Lemon.

ESTO: Who's she.

MARZ: Bitch makes yoga pants for people to wear in Starbucks.

ESTO: Why the fuck they wanna wear yoga pants in Starbucks?

MARZ: 'cause they telling everybody they going to yoga next.

ESTO: Who the fuck cares?

MARZ: The other people wearing yoga pants. I'm pulling coffee and all I hear is these ladies in they yoga pants talking 'bout they Boot Camp class. I'm like -- I was in the Navy -- I'll put a boot in they ass for half what these mutherfuckers chargin' 'em. Hung a flier -- now I'm a Boot Camp instructor for 'bout sixteen pairs of yoga pants.

ESTO: That's awesome man.

HOODY: That's bullshit that's what that is.

(*Marz notices the letters on the table.*)

MARZ: Looks like y'all got a little mail. (*Looks at the letter.*) How bad? (*No one answers.*) That bad. Whole hood gettin' hit. Some bills almost triple last year. Only going up from here. Big ass article about it in the Trib - not that any y'all gonna read it. Y'all remember Dookie?

ESTO: Joliet.

MARZ: Five to eight with good behavior.

HOODY: 'Cause he was stupid.

MARZ: 'Cause he was broke. Wasn't his fault.

HOODY: Here we go, who you gonna blame now?

ESTO: White people.

MARZ: Dookie was living here since we was kids and he ain't never jacked no cars. But then all the people from Lakeview start movin' in because they feelin' adventurous and shit. And guess what - a lot of them was white -- and Dookie was down with that for a while. It was all good. He was even hitting that white girl for a while.

ESTO: Sheila.

MARZ: Right and she was fine, too. But then, after a while, rent goes up and he can't afford to live in his own neighborhood, 'cause it ain't his neighborhood no more. It's theirs and he don't belong. So they evict his ass. Next thing you know his little white girlfriend is gone. She ain't about to be dating no homeless, pissed off brother, and before you know it he's sleeping under the Edens talking to pigeons like they was his kids. Then one day some other white girl come driving down the street in her brand new Beamer. She stops at the light and when he looks into her eyes, he sees everything he's lost. So instead of washing her windshield, Dookie decides he's gonna take somethin' back. Next thing you know, he's in lock up at County. Simple economics. (*To Hoody*) Maybe if you actually read some of your textbooks, you'd know this shit.

D: Dookie jacked a car. That ain't economics. That's a felony.

MARZ: That's reality. Y'all ain't never gonna learn are ya? I told you the shit's changin'. Y'all like dinosaurs, and it's gettin' cold out there. Time to wake your black Jurassic asses up. Look next door.

ESTO: Whatever man, that's one building.

MARZ: That's three families they kicked out that apartment so they could build one house. How you like your new neighbors? I hope a lot 'cause they dropped $350,000 to live here. That's why your tax bill's all jacked up.

HOODY: Ain't nobody gonna pay three fifty to live here.

MARZ: That's the point. They dropped three fifty 'cause they bettin' here ain't gonna be here for long.

ESTO: How you know they paid three fifty?

MARZ: Yummy. He hung dry wall over there for six months.

ESTO: I thought Yummy was a pimp.

MARZ: Yummy is a pimp.

ESTO: What kind a pimp hangs dry wall?

MARZ: The kind that set up shop in the middle of a recession. Had all his bitches spackling the bathrooms too. Yummy and his girls had to get creative to make their dollars. That's what I'm doing.

ESTO: Hear that Hoody?

HOODY: Just get y'self a job Lover Boy.

(*Esto exits.*)

D: Marz - we ain't going anywhere.

MARZ: Alright, say you find a way to make your bill this year. Ain't no way you gonna, but say you do. What you gonna do next year, and the year after that when you get reassessed again? This ain't no one time shot. People want return on their investment, so they bringin' everything with them - Baby Gap, Montessori fuckin' Whole Foods.

D: Good. Bout time. They selling Slims and Vodka on every corner but try and find a grape that ain't soda round here.

MARZ: That Whole Foods comes, folks like you and me is asked to leave.

(Marz takes the letter out of Hoody's hands and presents it to D. D grabs it out of his hands.)

D: You remember my momma Marz? Her last year, when she got really bad, she had to keep scoring to stop shaking. So we moved. Constantly. You remember Hoody.

HOODY: I remember hunting all over the damn hood to find you.

D: Twenty-eight. Slept in twenty-eight different beds that year - shelters, church basement, the park. I know because for my twelfth birthday I got a pack of real colored pencils from Pastor Hatch at the toy drive and I decided I was gonna be an artist. So I drew every bus stop and every boyfriend's couch. I still have 'em. Twenty-eight shaky sketches of places we had to call home every night. Then one morning momma stopped moving all together. And so did I. Came here. Hoody's momma - *(gesturing toward Marz)* your momma -- gave me number twenty-nine for a night. And I never left. Haven't spent a night outside this house ever since. First day you have a home is the last day you homeless. And I have a home. *(Looking to Hoody)* We have a home. *(Moving around the room collecting the phone, a pad of paper, a pen, etc.)* I'm gonna call down there. This ain't happening. Baby, look at me. Look at me. This ain't happening.

(D Kisses his cheek and exits.)

MARZ: *(In a husky female voice, imitating D)* Baby, look at me. Look at me. No wonder your ass so tired all the time.

HOODY: She'd kick your ass.

MARZ: You don't think I know that?

(A beat. Hoody cracks a slight smile.)

HOODY: Thought you hated Starbucks.

MARZ: I do. That's why I work there.

HOODY: Selling five-dollar coffee to people on food stamps.

MARZ: Everybody else making money off this hood, I can too. This some Robin Hood shit goin' on right here.

HOODY: Who your boss?

MARZ: Andy.

HOODY: White boy?

MARZ: Ever known a brother named Andy? And he ain't my boss, he my bitch.

HOODY: Naw man, you the bitch and you don't even know it. You ain't no Robin Hood. You just a ho with dental.

MARZ: That's all right, we all hos. Least I'm a well paid ho with benefits, a bonus and a uniform that ain't got my name on it. Another six months I'll have enough cash saved to get somewhere the fuck out of here.

(*Hoody reacts -- smirks and shakes his head.*)

MARZ (CONT'D): That's all right Jiffy Lube, we all got to make the bank any way we can. It's cool. I'll let you change my oil some time. Tip your ass real good, too.

HOODY: Remember where your black ass is from, Junior.

MARZ: I know where I'm from. And I know when it's time to leave.

(*Marz gets up to go.*)

HOODY: Yeah you was always good at leaving. Ever since we was kids all you ever did was run --

35

(*Marz stops.*)

MARZ: And all you ever did was get in the way.

HOODY: And you damn lucky too. I got in the way of a light skinned boy from Pilsen once -- right between you and his nine mil -- you remember that, junior?

MARZ: I remember you was the fucking magical negro -- gets shot -- rises from the dead -- you were a neighborhood savior man. Thug hero. Everybody on your jock after that. I remember you lovin' that shit.

HOODY: And I remember you disappearing.

MARZ: Don't make no difference -- ain't nobody in this hood ever see me anyway.

HOODY: I come out the hospital. You disappear. Mamma dies - you disappear. Bills come in - you disappear. Old man comes back around looking for cash - you disappear. Look at you man - you still running away.

MARZ: 'Cause I went to school I was runnin? 'cause I got out the house? I was walking man - forward. You were standing so still it just looked like I was running. What you gonna do Hoody? (*A beat.*) What you should do is get the fuck out. They buying lots -- vacant lots -- for 250 a pop. There are real estate agents all over my Starbucks man. That's where they work -- I got three of them want to do a damn deal right now. We can sell, split the cash and move on. This our ticket out man.

HOODY: Wait, We? Now there's a we? Where was we when the basement flooded? Where the hell is we when the goddamn furnace blows out twice a winter. Ain't been no we for a long time. Only been you and me.

MARZ: Momma's gone, Hoody. So's the hood. We should be too.

HOODY: This my home. That may not mean much to you - not that any motherfuckin' thing does --

MARZ: Thug hero days is over man... you still trying to be the neighborhood savior and they ain't no neighborhood left to save.

HOODY: Yeah well least that's better than only trying to save your own ass all the time.

MARZ: That's all anyone can save, man.

HOODY: Yeah? And how's that working out for you player?

MARZ: I ain't dead yet.

HOODY: Yeah, well me neither.

(*Lights fade to black.*)

ACT I / SCENE 4: BATMAN

(*Lights up on Hoody and D at the picnic table in their yard huddled over an economics text book. She is helping him with his homework.*)

D: Naw, see -- what'd we say -- this a liability right? Liabilities is the shit you owe, not what somebody owes you. Now what side of the balance sheet that go on?

(*Hoody gestures to an area of his worksheet.*)

D (CONT'D): Right side -- boom -- there you go. Now where does Property, Plant and Equipment go?

HOODY: I have no goddamn idea.

D: Okay let's start with something easier. Where does cash go?

HOODY: The hell out my pocket.

D: C'mon Hoody, I got to get to my own class.

HOODY: I pulled a double today --

D: And you trying to pull bullshit now --

HOODY: I don't need no damn worksheet --

D: Just do your homework.

HOODY: I don't have the head for this shit D -- you know that -- school ain't never been my...

D: Stop right there Hoody. This is your thing. All right? You ain't stupid. You stubborn. Occasionally you a act a fool -- but you ain't stupid. You feel me baby? I don't do stupid. You a brilliant black man. Say it.

HOODY: I'm a brilliant black man.

D: Like you mean it.

HOODY: I'm a brilliant black man.

D: That's right. You are. You marrying me. (*She gets up, kisses him.*) I gotta get to my class -- I'm gonna make you some flash cards tonight. You finish this while I'm gone. (*Off his reaction.*) Hoody.

HOODY: I'll finish it.

(*D gathers her stuff and exits. Hoody takes a beat, makes sure she is gone, then reaches into his book bag and pulls out a comic book and a joint. He flips open the comic book, and lights up. A light fades up on Czar's yard. Czar enters his yard. He is wearing a yoga tank top and yoga pants, and is carrying a yoga mat. He lays the yoga mat down and proceeds to get into the downward dog position. Hoody picks his head up out of the comic, looks into the next yard and sees czar in a full downward facing dog. Czar notices he's being watched and looks over at Hoody... for a beat, their eyes lock - Czar in his yoga pose - Hoody in his chair with a smoke and comic book.*)

CZAR: Howdy neighbor.

HOODY: The fuck you doin' man?

CZAR: Yoga. Vinyasa yoga. April got me started on it to relieve stress.

HOODY: Shit work?

CZAR: No, not really.

(*Hoody walks over to the fence and holds out the joint, offering it to Czar.*)

HOODY: This does.

CZAR: I don't smoke weed. (*A beat.*) In front of April.

(*Czar takes a bigger hit than expected.*)

HOODY: That's what I figured.

(*Czar hands the joint back to Hoody.*)

CZAR: What's that. Superman?

HOODY: Batman.

CZAR: Reissue?

HOODY: Vintage. Only take it out the plastic -

CZAR: When you need to relax.

HOODY: Used to be the Avengers, then I had my Fantastic Four phase.

CZAR: Who doesn't.

HOODY: But Batman is cool, he just a normal dude, you know? He ain't got no super powers from outer space like Superman. He's got to work it. Survivor and shit.

CZAR: Exactly. I never got Superman.

HOODY: He a tight ass.

CZAR: But Batman always seemed like a cool dude.

HOODY: Plus he got a pimped out ride -

CZAR: And Cat Woman's like porn hot.

(*Hoody nods. Takes a hit.*)

CZAR (CONT'D): I uh, got rid of all my comic books to make room for the baby.

HOODY: Sold 'em?

CZAR: Pitched 'em. I just felt this need to purge. I've been clinically insane since April got pregnant.

HOODY: Baby's a blessing man. Been raising babies all my life. Soon as I got outta my diapers I started changing Marz'. Raised cousins, D's cousins, nephews, nieces. You ain't really done anything till you raised a kid. Save your life man.

CZAR: I realize I haven't really done anything. I'm just not sure a kid's going to fix that.

HOODY: Y'all wanted kids though, right?

CZAR: It was time. April's clock's been ticking for a while, and she was like, we're doing this.

HOODY: Aw shit --

CZAR: Exactly.

HOODY: Momma says you gonna make a baby -- you gonna make a baby.

CZAR: Which was awesome. Like random mid-day ovulation sex -- and I'm thinking this could go on for a while 'cause we usually aren't good at the things we try -- but then boom -- it happened. We got pregnant and suddenly April's ecstatic and I'm ecstatic 'cause I've never seen her so happy, but inside, I'm either feeling complete terror or nothing at all.

HOODY: Yeah, well it ain't really about you anymore is it?

CZAR: No. No, it's not. I guess I forget that sometimes.

HOODY: That baby comes along, he ain't gonna let you forget it.

CZAR: Save my life, right?

HOODY: Least save you from yourself. Kids have a way of simplifying things. You get up every day and do it. You don't have to think about it.

CZAR: You got wisdom, Courtney.

HOODY: We grow up fast in Garfield Park.

CZAR: Yeah, I been meaning to do that myself one day.

HOODY: Then do it. Get your head out your ass and go have your baby. He on his way man.

CZAR: Sounds way less dickish when you say it.

HOODY: Say what.

CZAR: Calling him him -- I do that too -- but assuming male gender without actually knowing the baby's sex can come off as misogynistic and offensive to the fetus -- which is fine -- but... what do you think?

HOODY: I think y'all think too damn much. The word him should not set you off like that. That shit ain't healthy.

CZAR: See that's what -- I think we need to spend more time together. April says we need to make friends here and you're making sense to me man.

HOODY: Must be the yoga.

CZAR: Think it's the weed.

HOODY: How'd ya'll hook up?

CZAR: Me and April? Hyperhidrosis.

HOODY: Hyper who?

CZAR: Excessive sweating. Me not her. In big meetings I had this sweating thing like I was moist for a year... so I went to get checked out and she worked in the doctor's office... and...

HOODY: Damn man, you pulled ass at the sweat doctor? You got game player.

CZAR: Yes -- I did pull ass at the sweat doctor - how about you and D?

HOODY: High school. Her momma was in bad shape.

CZAR: Sick?

HOODY: Yeah. Addict. Bad scene, so my momma sort of took D in. We hooked up for a while, then took some time off - and - then I figured it out.

CZAR: What?

HOODY: Shit don't work without her. Rest is history.

CZAR: You got the girl, the yard, Batman - you're set man.

HOODY: That's what I used to think, too. House was damn near paid off, now our taxes like another mortgage.

CZAR: Yeah I saw that article in the Trib. (*Beat.*) I'm sorry, man.

HOODY: What you sorry for? Don't be sorry for me. You doing what you supposed to be doin' - you takin' care of your family.

CZAR: But I'm fucking with yours --

HOODY: See, that's your problem right there. That's a white boy thing. Y'all can't even enjoy the fact that you stepped up and bought a house.

CZAR: Well, it's kinda hard when you see the repercussions.

HOODY: Fuck repercussions. See brothers know how to handle success. You think Jay Z feelin' guilty 'bout his mansion in the Hamptons? Hell, no. There's a reason they ain't no black Kurt Cobains.

CZAR: It's called having a conscience.

HOODY: Yeah well conscience is expensive. This about survival, using what you got - taking care of your own - Batman versus Superman.

CZAR: If that's the case, then it's simple -- sell it. Easy. Done. Make a pile of cash, grab D, go start again somewhere else.

HOODY: Can't do that.

CZAR: Why not?

HOODY: I don't know.

CZAR: Yes you do. Your conscience won't let you do it. Maybe you're a little whiter than you think.

(*A beat.*)

HOODY: Yeah, well I still ain't doin' no yoga.

CZAR: Yeah - well, that's what I said too.

(*Hoody walks away from the fence, sits back down, lights a cigarette and resumes reading his comic book. Czar resumes his yoga pose. Lights fade to black.*)

ACT I / SCENE 5: BOOT CAMP

(*Lights up on Marz. Standing at attention are Spence and Barb in matching sweat suits. Spence is wearing protective sport goggles.*)

MARZ: Good morning, ladies. Welcome to Boot Camp Class. I am here to ruin y'alls day before you go to brunch at fuckin' Nookies. You feel me? Next three hours y'alls asses is mine. Anybody think they can't handle this shit, best get the fuck out now.

(*Spence begins to take off his sport goggles.*)

BARB: Spence.

(*Spence begins to put the sport goggles back on.*)

MARZ: What's your name Milky Way?

SPENCE: (*Smirking*) Spence.

MARZ: Something funny, Spencer?

SPENCE: No. I mean yes but... no.

MARZ: Wait up - hold on now. You address me as sir. You got that snowflake?

SPENCE: (*Motions for Marz to come closer, then quietly continues*) Look man, I get it, I'm in advertising, I understand this is all part of your brand identity and all that -- that's why we're here - it's great - but you might want to y'know -- just tone it down a bit, all right?

MARZ: So I should tone it down?

SPENCE: Yeah -- I mean.... we're in a park -- there are like toddlers learning how to swim over there. I mean I like what you're doing -- just maybe a bit less that's all.

MARZ: (*Quietly and right in Spence's face*) I'm gonna tell you a little secret Spencer, okay? This shit's for real man. Y'all picked the wrong motherfuckin' class. This ain't no Disney -fied, cardio-funk bullshit. I'm a militant mutherfucker and I enjoy this shit. You feel me player?

SPENCE: I feel you.

MARZ: Sir.

SPENCE: I feel you. Sir.

MARZ: Good. So why you here today Spencer?

SPENCE: We had a Groupon for another class that expired so—

MARZ: Naw man -- you tell me why you really here, Spencer!

SPENCE: We saw your ad in Starbucks and...

MARZ: And?!

SPENCE: My wife told me to come! Sir.

MARZ: You do everything your wife tells you to do?

(*Spence looks to Barb. She shakes her head "No."*)

SPENCE: No sir.

MARZ: You a warrior, Nilla?

SPENCE: No sir. Art Director sir.

MARZ: The hell you art direct?

SPENCE: Cheese Chunkers sir.

MARZ: (*Suddenly changing his energy.*) I fuckin' love Cheese Chunkers, man.

SPENCE: Really? 'Cause we have some focus groups coming up. Seventy five bucks and all the cheese product you can eat.

MARZ: No shit.

SPENCE: Yeah it's only like an hour.

MARZ: What I gotta do.

SPENCE: Eat Cheese Chunkers and tell me if you like them.

MARZ: I can do that.

SPENCE: Then do it.

MARZ: Done.

SPENCE: And bring some friends too.

MARZ: Seventy-five dollars each?

SPENCE: Per person.

MARZ: All right Spencer, we'll talk after class, I'll hit you with my celly and shit.

BARB: Excuse me. I'm sorry, I don't mean to -- I never complain -- but we sort of paid for this and want the full... thing... so...

MARZ: The hell she talking about?

SPENCE: She's wants more bat shit crazy.

MARZ: (*Back into character*) That's good 'cause I'm 'bout to go off on this motherfucker (*To Spence*) You hear me Tube Sock?

SPENCE: Yeah -- that's -- just like that.

(Marz moves to Barb.)

MARZ: *(Right up in her face)* How 'bout you -- you got a name two percent?

BARB: It's Barbara Sir!

MARZ: *(To Spence)* I think she can kick your lily white ass Spencer.

(Then back to Barb.)

MARZ (CONT'D): You do all your homework today Cracker Barrel? You run all three miles before class?

BARB: Yes sir.

MARZ: Didn't walk any of 'em.

BARB: No sir.

MARZ: 'Cause if you lyin', the rest of the platoon gonna pay.

(Spence looks around. Realizes he is the rest of the platoon.)

MARZ: You hear that, Spencer? If she lyin', I'm gonna take it out your ass. Hope you brought lots of water.

SPENCE: She walked, Sir.

BARB: Spence!

SPENCE: She totally walked!

BARB: Really!?

SPENCE: Hey I'm not the one who didn't run her three miles!

BARB: Will you please grow some balls Spence!

SPENCE: Oh I've got balls, Barb!

BARB: That's like the opposite of balls --

SPENCE: Look I am not gonna be sacrificed to Full Metal Jacket over here because your thighs were chafing!

BARB: You said you wanted to take this class!

SPENCE: I say lots of things I don't mean! It's called being married!

(*Marz blows his whistle.*)

MARZ: Ho - ho - hold on a second -- we gonna have to hug this shit out right here. Now I don't care whose thighs was rubbin' or whose balls is shrinkin'. Y'all got to feel the love, all right? Y'all lucky - look at you -- y'all got your family, little matching sweat suits and shit. Hug your man baby doll. That's right. Show your warrior some ba-dunk-a-dunk. There you go Spencer, grab that ass man - there you go - see y'all feel better? All right - now go get your mouth guards -- it's gonna get a little rough.

(*Lights fade to black.*)

49

ACT I / SCENE 6: B CUP, B STUDENT

(Lights fade up on April in a black hooded sweatshirt.)

APRIL: I am invisible. Been invisible all my life. When I was a kid I could go days, weeks, without being seen. Dirty brown dishwater hair and flat-ironed features wrapped in bad posture and functional shoes. A B-student with a B-cup from a sanitized suburb whose most extraordinary feat was a perfect attendance plaque and a Charlie hustle award at basketball camp. An upper middle-class, middle-of-the-bell-curve, too-quiet-to-be-tragic, too-boring-to-be-bulimic, forgettable flavor with an academic-alcoholic dad and a trophy-wife mom. So I tried to make myself be seen. From slut, to goth, to punk, to priss, to princess, to yogi. I hijacked identities and tried on personalities until they *had* to see me. Search and destroy, damn the torpedoes, cut your forearm with a kitchen knife and freak out a coffee-stained guidance counselor - be seen, be obscene, be witnessed, be intervened - until one day an ordinary man makes an extraordinary effort to make you feel smart and pretty. Enjoy seeing yourself through his eyes. Stop sleeping with his friends and start sleeping with him.

(Czar enters her light and begins to take off the black hooded sweatshirt. As she continues the monologue he pulls her hair back into a sensible pony tail and dresses her in a comfy/loose fitting top. The kind a woman might wear in the early months when she just begins to show.)

Get comfortable, get routine, get for granted, get honest about the fact that maybe you never stopped being invisible - until a little stick turns blue and 46 chromosomes turn you inside out for the whole world to see... with your thick hair and your bloody gums... until who you are, is no longer what you were. A tangible, fragile, dirty brown dishwater B-student, B-cup - *(A beat)* mommy, *(A beat)* - something singular and specific, authentic and committed - drunk with responsibility and dripping with identity.

50

Promise yourself it will be different. Find a house that looks nothing like the one you grew up in. Convince an ordinary man who makes an extraordinary effort that you are right... even if you aren't sure you are. (*A beat.*) Because for once, you need a place to be seen.

(*Lights fade to black.*)

ACT I / SCENE 7: HOUSEWARMING GIFT

(*Czar is working on the crib. Spence is watching. It is late evening. They are in the yard.*)

SPENCE: Y'know, there are directions in the box there.

CZAR: How do you not know how to do this --

SPENCE: It was three years ago --

CZAR: You called a guy didn't you?

SPENCE: Of course I called a guy -- if I didn't it would have looked like this --

CZAR: Just thought you would have wanted that moment of actually building your son's --

SPENCE: It's from IKEA. I don't know what kind of Little House on The Prairie daddy fantasy you have in your head - but guys aren't running around cutting down trees and forging their own steel to make cribs. Tyler loved this thing -- he didn't care who built it -- by the way a Diaper Genie's not a real genie.

CZAR: We sell mints.

SPENCE: Naughty mints.

CZAR: And fake cheese.

SPENCE: Cheese product.

CZAR: That's our life's work.

SPENCE: That's our job.

CZAR: That's why I want to build the crib.

SPENCE: Okay don't be angry ad-guy.

CZAR: I'm not any kind of ad-guy.

SPENCE: That make you feel better when you do that?

CZAR: Do what.

SPENCE: Ironic detachment is not transcendence. Hating something you do and still doing it isn't noble. It's pouting.

CZAR: What we do is bullshit. Being a dad isn't. This may be the only significant thing I ever do.

SPENCE: Well that doesn't put too much pressure on your kid. If you think any of this actually matters... you have one job -- keep 'em safe.

CZAR: I just think that when you're a dad you should --

SPENCE: You're not a dad -- you're like four months from being a dad -- you have no idea what matters --

CZAR: This matters.

SPENCE: Building a crib.

CZAR: Having a kid.

SPENCE: So you're freaking out.

CZAR: Yes!

(*A beat of release.*)

SPENCE: Oh well that's -- okay -- now I get it.

CZAR: I'm freaking out --

SPENCE: You need to build this crib --

CZAR: Exactly.

SPENCE: This is like your -- sanity -- spilled all over the yard—

CZAR: That's what I'm saying—

SPENCE: See this is good—

CZAR: This is not good.

SPENCE: No this is -- okay here's the deal -- you're not gonna be the father you imagine in your head. That's not how it works.

CZAR: And how does it work.

SPENCE: You're just... the dad you become. And once you're in -- you're in. You get this -- caveman daddy thing -- you'll do anything to protect that kid -- and... not screw the whole thing up too badly. Then one day you see them out in the world and -- they're doing good -- and at least for a moment they can make you -- less... cynical than you thought you could be.

CZAR: Sounds kinda great.

SPENCE: It is kinda great. Don't worry man -- every guy has that freak out moment where --

CZAR: Where he finds a guy sleeping on his porch?

SPENCE: Again? (*Off Czar...*) The guy just --

CZAR: Sleeps on our porch.

SPENCE: Like every night?

CZAR: Not every night but -- he's harmless --

SPENCE: And how do you know that?

CZAR: April told me.

SPENCE: Okay did you at least call the --

CZAR: No - we talked to him -- that's what we do -- we talk to the people who sleep on our porch 'cause we're building community. You don't call the cops -- you talk.

SPENCE: Yeah that makes sense. In Schaumberg we arrest them - but that's -- another way to go --

CZAR: At this point I just want to --

SPENCE: Build the crib.

CZAR: Yeah.

SPENCE: And what about the --

CZAR: Across the alley? Oh business seems to be good.

SPENCE: Well the economy's picking up.

CZAR: It's like Wal-Mart for crack heads --

SPENCE: And April's not nervous about all this?

CZAR: If she is, she doesn't tell me.

SPENCE: She's doing a thing.

CZAR: We're doing a thing.

SPENCE: You guys do a lot of things.

CZAR: Yes we do.

(April enters the yard from the house with her tools.)

APRIL: How's it coming?

SPENCE: He's a natural.

APRIL: Czar, do you just want me to do it?

SPENCE: She's way better at this that you.

CZAR: I'm fine.

SPENCE: He's not fine, he's freaking out--

CZAR: I've got this. I'm good.

APRIL: Or we can just use the one from next door, D said that-

CZAR: I'm building a crib.

SPENCE: He'll get past this. Super Dad phase ends right around that first neck shit. (*To Czar*) That's when the poopy shoots up their backs like a Super Soaker. Recycling's blue, right?

(*Czar nods. Spence grabs the cardboard box from the crib and heads toward the recycling bin.*)

SPENCE (CONT'D): April is my wife actually helping in there or is she just avoiding me --

APRIL/CZAR: She's been on the phone./She's avoiding you.

(*He tosses the box into the recycling bin and stops in his tracks.*)

SPENCE: Hey, you guys might want to check this out.

CZAR: I've seen the recycling bin, it's great.

SPENCE: Think someone had a little party back here.

(*Czar and April join Spence by the fence. They all look at something on the ground. Czar grabs a napkin and picks up a small pipe.*)

CZAR: That's great -- that's...

SPENCE: Might be your Wal-Mart buddies --

CZAR: (*Continuing to April*) See, this is what I was talking about --

APRIL: Let me see it --

CZAR: If they come into our yard -- that's just -- that's crossing the line --

APRIL: Were they in the recycling --

SPENCE: On the grass by the --

CZAR: In our yard.

APRIL: Someone could have tossed them over the fence --

CZAR: Or they could have been smoking crack fifteen feet from where we sleep --

APRIL: Let's just clean it up --

CZAR: From where our kid's gonna sleep --

SPENCE: There's another one --

CZAR: Of course what fun would it be to smoke crack in my yard by yourself, you need a buddy to --

SPENCE: Did you guys hear anything back here last night?

CZAR: I hear things every night -- there's constantly people in the alley.

APRIL: Okay don't overreact --

CZAR: Actually I think this is a great time to overreact -- that's a crack pipe.

APRIL: You don't know it's a crack pipe.

CZAR: You're right - it's a whistle.

(*Barb enters.*)

BARB: Ty bit a kid at Wiggle Worms.

SPENCE: What?

BARB: Our son. Bit another child. At Wiggle Worms.

SPENCE: With his mouth?

BARB: That's how you bite Spence, yes.

(*This next sequence happens simultaneously between both couples.*)

BARB/SPENCE:
    S: Our kid's a biter?
    B: Turned my phone on and there's like five e-mails from this afternoon -- *(Scrolling through her e-mails)* frantic Polish nanny -- crazed Lawyer mom --
    S: The mom called us?

APRIL/CZAR:
    A: We knew coming into this that things like this could happen --
    C: You knew we'd be finding these in our yard? -- I didn't know that --
    A: We knew there was going to be the occasional issue --
    C: It's been non-stop issues --

(*Spence breaks the sidebars and addresses the group.*)

SPENCE: Okay - they have crack whistles -- we have a biter -- we should go -- we need to -- yeah.

(*He and Barb start to leave.*)

BARB: Hold on. Wait --

SPENCE: What.

BARB: There's one from his teacher.

SPENCE: What'd she say?

BARB: (*Still reading the e-mail*) They did a conflict resolution during circle time. Ty apologized to the other boy -- in Spanish -- and the whole class journaled about it. (*She hits a button on her phone and puts it in her purse. Quietly to Spence*) This is why we live in Schaumburg.

APRIL: For the Spanish circle time.

BARB: I mean I get it -- our property taxes are -- (*gesturing*) -- but that's how you get an assistant instructor at Wiggle Worms with a dual masters degree in child psychology and conflict resolution.

APRIL: Isn't that a little --

SPENCE: Yes. It is. You guys are better off down here with less journaling and less dual masters degrees.

APRIL: There are actually a lot of resources here for kids.

SPENCE: Totally -- I'm not saying you don't have a lot of re-sources for kids.

APRIL: Actually you... did just sort of say that.

BARB: For us it makes sense -- biting thing aside, Ty's like this really sweet, sensitive --

SPENCE: Sort of nerdy --

BARB: Sort of nerdy... he's that kid... and we wanted to give him the chance to stay sweet and --

CZAR: (*Toward April*) Safe.

BARB: For us, Schaumburg wasn't a punch line.

APRIL: No. Just for everyone else.

BARB: I'm sorry -- I don't think I need to apologize for living in Schaumburg.

CZAR: You don't.

BARB: Just because I'm white and live in a suburb doesn't mean I'm a less authentic human being --

CZAR: You're not.

BARB: We had more foreclosures last year than Lakeview -- and Tyler's best friend is Iranian so --

CZAR: We get it -- that's --

BARB: Maybe I'm not the cool urban mommy or whatever but I'm not finding crack whistles in my yard –

SPENCE: Okay - we should probably --

APRIL: That's great -- you like the suburbs.

BARB: I don't like The Suburbs. I like my home -- and my street -- and my fucking Wiggle Worms class!

(*Hoody enters his yard.*)

HOODY: Hey y'all -- I know you probably drinking your white wine and shit -- kicking up your heels and partying or whatever but --

SPENCE/BARB/APRIL/CZAR:
S: No we're not -- no heel kicking, it was...

B: We were just talking... then Ty bit the other child... not a party, no.

C: Sorry man we just -- the crack pipe got everybody --

A: We're done. We're not -- yeah.

HOODY: It's just that D's sleeping -- she gotta big test early tomorrow morning so... And you know -- we just try to keep the block quiet, so maybe y'all can just... (*he gestures*)

SPENCE/BARB/APRIL/CZAR:
S: That makes total sense, I mean you wanna be --
B: We do the same thing in Schaumburg... Quiet hours are... good.
C: You gotta tell that to the guys across the alley --
A: We're sorry -- tell D good luck on the -- test.

(*Hoody smiles and nods, exits.*)

SPENCE: We're gonna -- yeah.

(*Spence and Barb exit. Czar moves back to the crib and begins working on it again. April approaches.*)

CZAR: If we're staying here -- we need do something.

APRIL: We're staying here.

CZAR: Then we need to do something.

(*End of Act I.*)

ACT II / SCENE 1: FOCUS GROUP

(*Lights up on Esto, D, Hoody and Marz seated on folding chairs in two rows. They chat/goof for a beat until Czar and Spence enter. Czar is carrying several boxes of Cheese Chunkers and Spence is holding an armful of poster boards.*)

CZAR: Hi, everybody. I'm Brian Czarpinski and this is my partner, Spencer Dillaway.

D: We know who you are.

CZAR: It's for the camera.

ESTO: We on camera?

CZAR: Yes.

ESTO: Can I do a rap?

CZAR: No.

SPENCE: I'd first like to thank Marz for bringing so many folks out to tonight's focus group. Czar you wanna --

CZAR: Okay sure... to give you a quick top-line on today's qualitative, we are the creative team behind the Cheese Chunkers campaign. Are any of you familiar with the Chunker campaign?

(*No response.*)

SPENCE: Don't be shy.

(*No response.*)

CZAR: Okay, low unaided awareness - no that's a good thing, that's fine, it's actually better 'cause outside opinions are what we're looking for.

SPENCE: We are going to pick your brains on how we can make our advertising and communications platform more relevant and engaging to the key African-American slash (*he nods to Esto*) "Urban" Chunker market that has traditionally been underdeveloped and provides a significant conquesting opportunity, both in terms of market share and top-of-mind awareness among this key demographic.

(*A beat.*)

HOODY: So you tryin' to find out if black people like cheese.

SPENCE: Product. It's cheese product. We can't - legally call it cheese.

CZAR: Okay, any other questions before we get started?

D: When do we get our $75?

SPENCE: At the end. (*Gesturing to another raised hand*) Yeah?

ESTO: When's the end?

CZAR: Just show them Curtis.

SPENCE: Right, okay. We'd like you to meet someone today. Actually not someone... something. Something the world has never before seen. (*Grabbing a board and holding it up to the group*) Introducing Curtis the Cheese Chunker - the cheese rapper that doesn't come in a cheese wrapper.

(*He holds up a poster board.*)

CZAR: Just let it wash over you.

(*There is a beat of silence, then they all bust out laughing.*)

SPENCE: Okay - let's get some reactions to Curtis. Be honest. Do you find him relatable? Is he street enough to be considered a "gangsta" snacking alternative?

MARZ: Damn that's like a whole bucket of fucked-up right there.

ESTO: Y'all like even know any black people?

D: Why's he grabbin' himself like that?

SPENCE: We can dial down the "crotch clutch" if it distracts from the appetite appeal.

MARZ: He look like a big yellow turd to me.

ESTO: That's right, Turd-Pac.

(*ESTO and MARZ laugh and slap hands.*)

MARZ: I think he should be flashing gang signs like a crazy ass thug turd.

SPENCE: Y'know I'm not sure we want our turd to go full-on thug.

CZAR: Unless thug is a good thing.

SPENCE: Let's probe on that -- how dangerous do we want Curtis to be? Is he Old Dirty Bastard cheese? Suge Knight Cheese --

HOODY: Who supposed to eat this?

CZAR: Kids, primary target is 6-10 year-old African-Americans with some spill into the tweens and teens segment.

HOODY: How much do these cost?

CZAR: They'll retail at a premium price point - around $5.99 per pack.

SPENCE: But there will be a loyalty program where kids collect "curd" points for premium Chunker wear.

D: They good for kids?

SPENCE: Good is a relative thing.

MARZ: So, relative to crack, they good.

SPENCE: This isn't meant to be health food, this is fun-shaped finger food for kids when they come home from school and—

D: So y'all are selling over-priced fake cheese to black kids.

SPENCE: It's more complicated than that, see -

CZAR: Spence, stop. *(To D.)* That's exactly what we are doing.

HOODY: And this is your job.

SPENCE: Least for the time being.

(Hoody reacts, gesturing and shaking his head.)

MARZ: Yo man -- I say do your thing Spencer. *(Off Hoody's reaction)* What you gonna get all righteous on this shit man? You think these the only motherfuckers doing this? This happening every day. Ain't no different than P-Diddy sellin' his hundred-dollar vodka to all the little Esto's running round the hood.

ESTO: Yo man that's good-ass vodka.

MARZ: See. They robbin' the hood just like y'all's heroes -- same damn thing -- ain't no worse. This ain't got nothing to do with black or white, it's just about the green.

HOODY: Don't make it right --

MARZ: Ain't talking 'bout what's right -- I'm talkin' 'bout what's real.

HOODY: They ain't nothing real about this shit -- it's cheese product.

CZAR: Okay I think we're done.

SPENCE: Hold on.

CZAR: Spence --

SPENCE: You're missing the point -- this isn't food.

HOODY: No -- we got that point.

SPENCE: It's entertainment.

D: I don't want to break it to y'all, but this ain't Disney World.

SPENCE: Actually that's exactly what it is. (*A beat.*) I wanna know something. How many of you have been to Disney World?

(*No one raises their hand.*)

SPENCE (CONT'D): And why's that?

ESTO: Fuckin' expensive man.

SPENCE: That's right -- it's real fuckin' expensive. Why? Because they sell magic. And magic ain't cheap. But just because you don't have the cash to go to Disney World -- doesn't mean you still don't wanna give your kids a little bit of magic once in a while... see that sparkle in their eyes. They're your kids.

HOODY: They our kids -- but they ain't going to no Disney World.

SPENCE: Exactly. And that's okay because Disney World isn't a place -- it's an idea. It's about making your babies smile and making you feel better about being a parent. That is its power -- and that's exactly what these do. In some small, tiny way -- they bring out a little bit of that magic... that joy... so on a snowy Wednesday in Garfield Park when these kids run home from school 'cause they're too afraid to walk -- they may be a million miles away from The Happiest Place on Earth -- but you can still open a box of these and -- for an instant -- make your kid feel special... and safe. For five dollars and ninety-nine cents. Now you can rag on these all you want. I'm not saying they're the end-all be-all... and I'm not saying to eat 'em every day... and I'm certainly not saying they're health food. But I am saying that there's a whole lot more in this box than cheese product. And that's what you're buying.

CZAR: Okay... any other questions.

(*Every hand goes up.*)

CZAR (CONT'D): Other than when you get your seventy-five dollars.

(*Every hand goes down.*)

CZAR (CONT'D): (*To Spence*) We good?

SPENCE: Relative to crack.

CZAR: Checks are at the front desk.

(*The group gets up to get their checks. Lights fade to black.*)

ACT II / SCENE 2: HEAR ME

(The stage is dark. A tight spotlight comes up on a figure wearing a black hooded sweatshirt. We see that it is D.)

D: I am invisible. Been invisible all my life - spent years moving through the shadows and cracks of broken men and angry boys too proud to ask for help, and too arrogant to say thank you when you give it to them anyway. Fierce, black and strong, I watched the pride lion puff up and go out into the wasteland only to come home and explode. Fantastic, tragic fireworks filled with bravado and machismo, his wives and daughters circling his fire, soothing his burns, stroking his face, and whispering sweet relief between the pounding in his ears.

(Hoody enters her light and pulls the hood back off her face. A beat later he takes the sweatshirt off her shoulders, puts an industrial cleaning smock on her, and leaves her light.)

D (CONT'D): And when the noise stops, and the darkness fills the room, I show up, like I always do, in the shadows and the silence, with a bucket and a mop. Bandage a baby brother's bloody hand. Steady daddy as he pisses Hennessey into a jelly jar 'cause he's too drunk to stand. I clean up the glass. Lock the door. And turn off the light. Because I do not need to be seen. I need to be heard. From baby cry to lullaby, life isn't what you see. It is what you hear. And when you a two-month cocoa brown baby girl left alone in a second story walk up - you need to be heard. So I cried until they heard me. And when your cousin takes you under the freeway, and no one can hear you over the roar of the trucks on The Kennedy, you need to be heard. So I screamed until they found me, until I found my own voice. Simple and clear. Louder than you'd expect. And it was fierce... almost beautiful. But now, I have gone silent once again. Six community meetings and three trips to the Cook County Assessor and I still cannot be heard. Two loan officers and a local news reporter, and I still cannot be heard.

A half hour alone with a tax bill and an alderman... and I still cannot be heard. So every night I come home tired and hoarse -- having lost my voice again -- to say good night to a proud man who always listens but doesn't always hear.

(*Lights fade to black.*)

ACT II / SCENE 3: SHADOWS AND STAINS

(*D walks into the next scene wearing the blue commercial cleaning uniform. Hoody is seated in his chair. She sees Hoody and pauses.*)

HOODY: Why ain't you told me.

D: Ain't nothing to tell.

HOODY: Why don't you try.

D: I'm picking up some shifts.

HOODY: How many?

D: Many as I can get.

HOODY: How you doing that and going to class. (*A beat.*) Aw hell no.

D: Not now Hoody.

HOODY: What do you mean not now -- I

D: I gotta go to work --

HOODY: This ain't your job D.

D: This ain't your call.

HOODY: Naw -- hell no - I ain't about to let you --

D: Let me what. Now you let me do things? That's how it works now - you let me do things now?

HOODY: That's not what I'm --

D: 'Cause I didn't realize I hadda ask permission from you every time I --

HOODY: You need to be in school D - that's your future.

D: I need to be makin' dollars. That's my reality.

HOODY: All for some bullshit tax bill.

D: It ain't bullshit Hoody - this for real. It's time we get real about this thing okay? We gonna -- we gonna lose this house if we don't do something. So I'm doing something.

HOODY: Yeah you quitting.

D: No. I'm surviving. That's what we good at, remember?

(*A beat.*)

HOODY: How you even find this job. And don't say Marz.

D: Fine I won't say it.

HOODY: Goddamn. You serious.

D: He got me in.

HOODY: So now you cleaning his Starbucks.

D: I'm cleaning a bunch of Starbucks.

HOODY: Oh I bet he's loving that.

D: I don't care if he is. Neither should you.

HOODY: He needs to stay the fuck out our business --

D: He's your brother.

HOODY: That don't give him any goddman right to --

D: I asked him. Hoody. Okay? I -- asked -- him.

HOODY: You asked Marz. I told you I'd figure something out.

D: I know you did.

(*Cross fade to Czar and April's yard. April is significantly more pregnant. She is sitting at the picnic table attempting to sew (albeit poorly) something that approximates a quilt using the swatch D has given her. Upstage we see that a portion of the house is now covered in graffiti. Czar is taking photos of the gang symbols with his smart phone.)*

APRIL: You realize that's the fourth time you took that shot.

CZAR: They like detail in the reports.

APRIL: Then they must love your reports.

CZAR: At this point they tolerate my reports.

APRIL: You've got patrols coming by twice a day - the camera's up in the intersection -- the alderman knows you by name.

CZAR: (*Gesturing to the graffiti*) And we still get this.

APRIL: Maybe that's why we get this. (*A beat.*) People know we constantly call.

CZAR: Because there's constantly a reason to call. It's common sense.

APRIL: But it's not community. I want a home Czar.

CZAR: We have a home.

APRIL: We have a house.

CZAR: I don't know how to change that.

(*She moves to him, takes the camera phone out of his hands.*)

APRIL: Okay -- I think we need to stop the forensics for one night and focus on each other. Remember us?

(*A beat as she moves closer.*)

CZAR: You mean like -- (*He gestures.*)

APRIL: Actually I was hoping we could talk.

CZAR: No -- No. No talk. All we do is talk. I think we should focus on each other with a little date night.

APRIL: This will take two minutes.

CZAR: So will date night. That was a joke it won't take that long.

APRIL: I'm serious Czar, I think we should talk.

CZAR: About what.

APRIL: This. Look at us -- we didn't used to be so...

CZAR: Scared?

APRIL: Alone.

CZAR: Yeah well we also didn't used to be so pregnant and so in Garfield Park.

APRIL: We're not in Garfield Park -- we're in our own little bubble and in case you haven't noticed, building a bigger fence isn't the answer --

CZAR: Then what is.

(*A beat.*)

APRIL: What if we help?

CZAR: What, next door?

(She gestures.)

CZAR (CONT'D): We're not gonna pay their tax bill.

APRIL: We could help. We'd be helping ourselves -- they're good neighbors. Maybe they can help us -- they're actually nice to us --

CZAR: You mean when we're not finding crack pipes and graffiti?

APRIL: He totally keeps an eye on our house when we're not here.

CZAR: For all we know, they could be a part of this.

APRIL: If it were other friends of ours -- we'd help.

CZAR: If it were other friends of ours, they wouldn't ask.

APRIL: They didn't ask.

CZAR: Are they our friends?

APRIL: I hope so.

CZAR: I'm not sure that counts. He's a proud guy -- we're just gonna insult him.

APRIL: You don't know that.

CZAR: He's like this throwback to-to-to-- he's like this -- he doesn't sell things.

APRIL: What does that mean?

CZAR: It means he's nothing like me. I'd take the help. That's how I know he wouldn't.

(A beat.)

APRIL: What about her. She loves that house.

CZAR: We don't know them well enough to give them money.

APRIL: It'd be a loan.

CZAR: That's great -- and how do we collect payments if they're late? Who's gonna knock on their door and ask for the money? And how do we tell them that we don't have another five grand when their furnace goes out or their car breaks down and they need some more help? And how do we keep the whole neighborhood from thinking we have that kind of cash to throw around when we don't. We're barely surviving this mortgage as it is. I'm more concerned about us being able to stay here than them. At what point does this end -- how -- when -- do you become happy?

(A beat.)

APRIL: We're not going anywhere.

CZAR: These are gang symbols.

APRIL: I know what they are.

CZAR: This is the third time -- one more month our kid is in that house.

APRIL: We decided to live here.

CZAR: Yeah, I remember when you told me we decided that.

APRIL: You were the one who wanted a house.

CZAR: I just didn't want another condo where you have to put the crib in the kitchen.

APRIL: What you wanted to do was run to the suburbs like everybody else.

CZAR: And what's wrong with that?

APRIL: I'm your wife that what's wrong with it.

CZAR: It's not like we're cracking glow sticks and dropping ecstasy every night. You're in a book club for crissakes -- at this point we sort of belong in the suburbs.

APRIL: Don't tell me where I belong Czar --

CZAR: Great -- we can live here and our kids will be dropping F-bombs in pre-school and hiding one hitters their Hello Kitty knapsacks.

APRIL: You're right. I was twelve before I did that. And I didn't have sex until I was fifteen.

CZAR: We're not talking about you --

APRIL: Yes. We are. And I didn't even get pregnant until my Sophomore year -

CZAR: I know what happened --

APRIL: I'm sure the nurse at the clinic thought I was a late bloomer compared to those sluts from the city. Wouldn't it be great if our kids could experience the same thing? And as a bonus they'll grow up with a false sense of entitlement and an irrational fear of black people.

CZAR: So the "suburbs" are the reason you got knocked up at the Sadie Hawkin's Dance twenty years ago. The "suburbs" are why your dad drank, your mom checked out and your brother still doesn't have a job. It wasn't your neighborhood that was broken, April.

(*A beat.*)

CZAR (CONT'D): Look, I'm sorry - that's not --

76

APRIL: Stop.

CZAR: I didn't mean what I said.

APRIL: You rarely do.

(*April turns and exits into the house.*)

ACT II / SCENE 4: UNDERVALUED WHITE BOY

(*Lights fade up on Hoody in his yard. He is on the ground in a downward dog position. Exactly like Czar had done earlier. Esto enters and sort of examines Hoody's body position.*)

ESTO: If you're looking for your balls, they might be in your yoga bag.

HOODY: I gotta test tonight. Spent all week trying to get your ass an apartment instead of studying.

ESTO: So... you studying.

HOODY: I'm relieving stress.

ESTO: Perfect. I can help. C'mon man -- TV is very relaxing.

HOODY: Ain't watching no damn TV.

ESTO: Yo man, I'm gonna be on the news -- I don't want to miss it.

HOODY: This is my house, all right? You wanna watch TV, get your own damn house.

ESTO: I quit.

HOODY: That ain't news.

ESTO: No. But after I quit, I dropped ass in the middle of Red Lobsters.

HOODY: Shut the fuck up.

ESTO: Dropped my Dockers and sat down on the salad bar.

HOODY: Sat your naked ass down on the salad bar?

ESTO: Watch the news you'll see.

HOODY: Watch it at your mom's.

ESTO: They shut off her cable.

HOODY: Again. Y'all just ghetto.

ESTO: Oh yeah, I forgot. When you gonna be on Cribs again, Kanye?

HOODY: I ain't gonna watch you act a fool.

ESTO: They're the fools man. That's why I quit.

HOODY: What, you too good to work at Red Lobsters?

ESTO: Yes. No. I don't know man, maybe.

HOODY: Red Lobsters' a fine establishment. You think anyone in this neighborhood gonna be able to eat shrimps anywhere else? I for one don't get much shrimp, but when I go to Red Lobsters, I eat the shit out them little shrimps. Where you take your brother for eighth grade graduation?

ESTO: Red Lobsters.

HOODY: Where you go for your cousin's communion?

ESTO: Red Lobsters.

HOODY: Where your momma eat dinner Sunday after payday?

ESTO: Red Fuckin' Lobsters.

HOODY: That's right. Red Fuckin' Lobsters.

ESTO: You don't get it, man. They let me bus tables today.

(*This catches Hoody's attention.*)

HOODY: Wait, hold on -- they let you bus?

ESTO: Ain't even seen the front of the restaurant since I started -- just scraping shrimp every damn day - but today Hal's like, yo - cover your tats and you can fill water glasses.

HOODY: So you got promoted to water boy.

ESTO: Fucked up part is I been in the back so long I was actually nervous -- wasn't sure I could pour water into a glass.

HOODY: So you dropped your damn pants -

ESTO: Nah man I poured my damn water. I was on it too - dude takes a sip BAM! I hit him again. I was bringing bitches limes, asking if mutherfuckers wanted crushed ice or cubes, waving to punk-ass Julio who took over my shrimp scraping - then I get a four top with a bunch of kids from New Trier -- look like a catalogue from J Crew.

HOODY: Aw shit.

ESTO: I'm topping them off, big-ass chunk of ice gets stuck in the bottom of the pitcher, I try to shake it loose and the whole thing dumps on the dude's lap. Dude freaks. So now I got a cocky-ass North Shore sophomore with soggy balls all pissed off 'cause now his cheerleader ain't so impressed with him and his daddy's Beamer.

HOODY: So where's Hal?

ESTO: Exactly - where's Hal. I'm like dude keep it down. Hal hears and I am the fuck back scraping shrimp with Julio. I'm like yo man I'll dry you off - it's all good. But now he starts fucking with me in front of his buddies. He's like yo, Eminem, you missed a spot.

HOODY: Here it comes.

ESTO: Hoody. I'm on my hands and knees picking ice off the floor and this little cracker still calls Hal over. So I'm like fuck it - you want some dry pants - take mine mutherfucker - here they are. Took a little walk around the restaurant all gangsta style, one hand on my nutsack, one hand in the air. They called the cops. Channel seven showed up --

HOODY: Ho - they called the cops? They run your priors?

ESTO: Naw man, nothing. Big ass Pollock cops from the Southside -- they hate New Trier kids too -- thought the whole thing was hilarious. It was some whack shit. You'll see. I hadda do it man.

HOODY: You ain't hadda do nothing. You know how close you came to getting busted again, man? Guys like us can't afford to quit nothing. Ever.

ESTO: I'll be all right. I'm a player.

HOODY: You ain't no player. You just an undervalued white boy.

ESTO: Oh yeah, well what's that make you?

HOODY: Same thing, only black. Which makes me the only mother fucker in worse shape than you. I gotta go flunk a test.

(*Hoody begins to leave.*)

ESTO: Lots of ways to make dollars in this hood.

(*Hoody stops.*)

HOODY: What Esto, you wanna start dippin' again? Those days is over man, you retired. Cops are all over this hood now man -- we livin' in the high rent district -- soccer moms don't like dudes like you hanging on they corner. If you moving bags -- you gonna get busted. Or worse. Young thugs today shoot you in the face as soon as look at you. And for what? A Rocawear jersey and some Hennessey. Everybody wants to be J mother fucking Z - well, it ain't like that up in here. This ain't the Hills man, this Garfield Park so you better start getting Garfield smart -- or did you forget?

ESTO: I ain't forgot nothin'. You're the one that forgot how to hustle - you forgot everything, including me for nine months, two weeks and thirteen days --

HOODY: Who got you a job when you got out? Who you think drove your momma to visitation every damn week? Not to mention the lawyer I paid for -- shit I sent your ass cookies.

ESTO: They were Nilla Wafers man. They ain't even cookies - they're fuckin'... wafers.

HOODY: Just work your program and stay the fuck home man.

ESTO: I don't have a home.

HOODY: Then maybe you should get one!

(*A beat.*)

ESTO: Two years. Two fuckin' years I went to meetings, called my probation officer every goddamn day at 2:30... fuck I coached little league last summer. And for what. This is what I am, Hoody. I'll never be anything else. I've accepted that. And you know what? It feels good. You should try it sometime Hoody.

(*Esto exits. Hoody gathers up his books. He begins to exit the yard and Marz appears at the fence holding a large yellow envelope.*)

HOODY: You lost man?

MARZ: Just came by to drop this off. (*He holds up the large yellow envelope.*) It's a good offer.

HOODY: The fuck we get an offer?

MARZ: I was talking to one of the real estate agents that hangs out at Starbucks --

HOODY: You always talking --

MARZ: She wanted to see it --

HOODY: You showed the house.

MARZ: I brought her by to see it. (*Off Hoody's look...*) It's half mine man. She wants to buy it. Develop it herself.

HOODY: You mean knock it down.

MARZ: Maybe. Can't stay might as well get paid. All we gotta do is sign and get the fuck out.

HOODY: Get the fuck out.

MARZ: That's right -- get the fuck out.

HOODY: You just gonna keep running ain't ya? Where you going this time?

MARZ: LA.

HOODY: LA.

MARZ: Far as I can get from here.

HOODY: Know anybody out there?

MARZ: No.

HOODY: Then it'll be just like here.

MARZ: If it is, I'll go somewhere else.

(*A beat.*)

HOODY: All right then.

MARZ : All right then. (*A beat.*) Just pretend I had nothing to do with it and take a look. This ain't no old school crazy-ass Mississippi shit -- it's a contract. That's what you get when you starting a new adventure. Not a swatch. It's all there -- sixty forty. (*A beat.*) Thought you could use the extra ten percent. Get D back to cuttin' heads 'stead of cleaning coffee shops. Consider it the first ever Marz Coleman save-someone-other-than-his-own-ass scholarship fund.

(*Marz begins to exit.*)

HOODY: Yo man, I ain't no neighborhood savior. Never was one.

MARZ: Yeah well maybe I ain't no Robin Hood neither.

(*Marz turns to leave.*)

HOODY: Yeah but I can't do what you do. (*A beat.*) I don't know how.

(*A beat.*)

MARZ: I stopped.

HOODY: What?

MARZ: I stopped. Heard two shots - POP - POP. Turned around, saw you go down, and - I stopped running. Block was empty. Just that light-skinned boy from Pilsen still talking shit as he hopped the fence. Came back and you was out man. I could hear the sirens coming. Had just enough time to grab your stash and pack your chest with my Bulls jersey before the cops came and started asking questions and shit.

HOODY: That was you.

MARZ: Ruined my brand new Bulls Jersey too man. It was a Jordan and shit.

HOODY: You ain't never told me.

MARZ: It ain't never mattered.

HOODY: It all matters.

(*Marz holds the yellow envelope out to Hoody. Hoody does not reach out to accept it. Marz takes a beat then sets it on the picnic table in front of Hoody who exits. Lights fade except for a dim blue spot on Marz....*)

ACT II / SCENE 5: BLACK COFFEE

(The dim blue spot light remains on Marz as Barb, Spence, April and Czar form a semi-circle in the darkness around him.)

SPENCE: Hi I'd like a half caf, 2%, no foam, extra hot, two pump, triple shot venti dolce mochiatto with whip.

MARZ: And I'd like you to believe I actually listen to the shit you people say. This fuckin' coffee. Put it in a cup with some milk and sugar and drink the mutherfucker.

APRIL: Is this me?

MARZ: I have no goddamn idea. They all the same anyway, baby.

CZAR: Hi, I'd like to piss away a bunch of money in front of people who make $7.15 an hour.

MARZ: Great - would you like a sense of superiority with that?

BARB: Um, I think I'll go with some clueless denial, and- oh, how's your ignorance?

MARZ: Debilitating.

SPENCE: Perfect. Oh and can I get one of those little trays for my sense of apathy?

APRIL: Hi, I'm thinking I'm going to have something over-priced and unnecessary.

MARZ: And I'm thinking you're overpriced and unnecessary.

CZAR: Then instead of actually talking to you, I'm going to stand here and pretend to check messages.

MARZ: And I'm going to stand here and pretend that I don't know that.

BARB: Then to compensate for my complete lack of humanity, I'm going cheer like a schoolgirl when my drink comes -- feeling satisfied that I have my very own black coffee buddy.

MARZ: And I'm gonna... pour your coffee.

(*A beat. The light fades on everyone but Marz.*)

MARZ (CONT'D): And I'm gonna nod and smile and count my days and watch you look right through me like I ain't even here. (*Taking off his barista hat.*) And it's tight too 'cause when you young and you angry and you invisible... you get to watch. And learn. And next thing you know -- you beatin' these mutherfuckers at their own game and they don't even know what hit 'em. (*Taking off his barista apron.*) Can't catch what you can't see. And ain't nobody gonna see me. Throw my hood up over my head, eyes pushed way back deep inside, and poof, just disappear.

(*Marz exits. Lights down.*)

ACT II / SCENE 6: THE PARTY

(Lights up on D in April's yard on a cordless phone. She speaks in a hushed tone. April is at a picnic table cutting vegetables for the party, trying not to listen.)

D: *(Into the phone)* Willis. Danisha Willis. No I told you I'm his fiancée, I called last week and they said - no, the account is under Courtney Coleman. With a "C." Right. I know we're passed due, that's why I'm calling, but no one is able to -- no I won't hold -- I was on hold yesterday for thirty minutes and - I understand it's after five - but we have collection sending us letters 'cause y'all - no, it tripled, that's not an adjustment - that's what I've been trying to - so what are we supposed to - no, I'm still not a senior citizen or a disabled veteran. That's not an option less you want to give me your credit card. You're a district manager - I been calling two weeks to talk to YOU, Carol, 'cause you're supposed to be the one that can help -- No, see that's where you're wrong - we're talking about my home. You understand that Carol? I'm about to lose my home and you telling me to write a damn letter and hope the shit changes instead of getting' up off your ass and actually helping the people you getting' paid to serve. Well get used to it baby 'cause I'm just getting started. Talk to you tomorrow, Carol. *(D hangs up the phone, takes a breath, then turns to April.)* I'm sorry -- I don't usually - thanks for the phone.

APRIL: No problem - I'm glad we could --

D: I wouldn't have even asked but --

APRIL: D - it's OK. Really.

D: I should go. Y'all getting ready for your baby party.

APRIL: Stay. Please. You can help me with the salad.

(April moves a pile of fresh snap peas toward D. They begin snapping them and putting them into a big bowl.)

APRIL (CONT'D): D... if you ever need more than a phone... like if you ever want to talk or whatever -- Czar and I have been talking and... I dunno... I just haven't had a chance to meet many people here --

D: Who you wanna meet?

APRIL: Well nobody in particular -- it's more just -- this can be a hard place to be a part of if you weren't born here.

D: Why you here, April?

APRIL: What do you mean?

D: I mean why are you here?

APRIL: Well... lots of reasons. I think most of all, Czar and I wanted to --

D: That's the difference. Right there. People from this hood are here 'cause they have to be, not because they want to be.

APRIL: You don't want to be here?

D: I don't have the luxury of asking the question.

APRIL: Or maybe you're afraid to ask it.

D: You have no idea what I am afraid of.

APRIL: I know. That's why I'm asking.

D: April, I don't think this is going to be our Oprah moment.

APRIL: I'm not sure what that means.

D: It means thanks for the phone.

(*She snaps a few more beans then stops.*)

D (CONT'D): It means you have the nicest home I've ever seen... and I'm trying to figure out how not to lose the only one I've ever known... and right now I can't afford to make a phone call. I don't mean to disappoint you, but I ain't your soul sister. I ain't even your friend yet.

APRIL: What are you?

D: I'm your neighbor.

BARB (*OS*): Hey, you guys need anything back there?

APRIL: (*To Barb.*) We're fine. (*To D.*) And for the record I don't watch Oprah.

D: Thought all white women did.

APRIL: Yeah well you thought wrong.

(*Barb enters with napkins and appetizers.*)

BARB: April where do you want the apps?

D: Barb -- Oprah.

BARB: Oh my god I would totally make out with that woman.

APRIL: Doesn't mean she watches the show.

BARB: I haven't had time since Ty started soccer --

(*Czar and Spence enter with drinks.*)

CZAR: Okay drinks are served! (*We hear a baby cry coming from a baby monitor on the picnic table.*) And he's up.

APRIL: That's early for him.

CZAR: Ladies and gentlemen the guest of honor has awoke. (*To April*) You mind if I get him?

90

APRIL: Aw... I was gonna change him.

CZAR: You changed him last time --

APRIL: Yeah but --

SPENCE: Guys there's plenty more where that came from -- trust me -- plenty to go around.

(*April exits toward the house to get the baby.*)

APRIL: Be right back -- gotta go see my man.

CZAR: (*To April*) If you need help just -- I'm here.

(*Just then Hoody enters his own yard, then crosses into Czar's yard through a gate that no one has previously used.*)

HOODY: 'Sup people. 'Sup baby.

(*Czar, Spence and Barb greet Hoody.*)

D: Hey Baby.

CZAR: Hoody! Thanks for coming man.

HOODY: Brought some of my famous dirty rice. He hands the dish over to Czar.

BARB: That looks awesome.

HOODY: I made it spicy. (*To Spence*) And I brought these for y'all. (*He pulls out a pack of Cheese Chunkers.*) That's some fun-shaped-finger-food and shit.

(*Spence smiles, improvises a positive reaction.*)

HOODY (CONT'D): (*To Czar*) And this is for -- where's your boy?

CZAR: Pooping or sleeping.

HOODY: Well yo -- this here for him.

(*Hoody pulls a small piece of fabric from his back pocket and hands it to Czar.*)

CZAR: Swatch.

HOODY: Got little Chewbaccas on it and shit -- figured you got yourself a little homeboy -- he ain't gonna want no damn flowers on his quilt, so...

CZAR: That's -- thank you. Courtney. Thank you.

HOODY: Tradition man.

(*They shake hands and do a half man hug. April enters carrying an infant wrapped tight in a blanket.*)

APRIL: Somebody's still tired.

BARB/SPENCE/HOODY:
Ohhh there he is./Hey little man./There's homeboy.

(*They all react to the baby forming a semi-circle around April as they continue to improvise -- talking to the baby and trying to make him smile.*)

BARB: He is so cute --

SPENCE: You guys do good work --

D: Oh my God -- look at that fat baby!

APRIL: Is he fat -- 'cause in the book it said --

HOODY: That mean healthy. It's a black thing.

SPENCE: Then I am really healthy. That's a fat white guy thing.

(*Czar comes to April, she hands the baby off to him.*)

CZAR: C'mere big fella -- say hi Bri-Bri.

APRIL: Got him?

CZAR: I got him.

APRIL: Okay I'm gonna grab his woobie and I can't believe I just said that.

(*April exits into the house.*)

HOODY: Got y'self a Junior, huh.

CZAR: Yeah - never saw myself as a guy who'd name his son after himself -- but... I guess I am.

HOODY: Feels good though doesn't it.

(*Czar nods. So does Hoody.*)

CZAR: I just didn't want to name him something tragic and trendy.

SPENCE: For the record when we named him Tyler Jayden it was way less tragic and trendy.

BARB: (*To Spence*) You know I can hear when you speak.

(*April enters the yard from the house with the woobie and a big bowl of chips and salsa.*)

APRIL: Okay, who's ready for my husband's world-renowned pineapple salsa?

D: Y'all go first -- you the new mommy.

APRIL: I can't -- the chiles go right through the boobs -- not sure Bri-Bri is ready for Habaneros.

SPENCE: He's not but I am. (*Dips a chip in the salsa.*) So glad I'm not breast feeding.

APRIL: We have plenty to eat and drink so help yourselves. (*Everyone digs in.*)

CZAR: So is Esto gonna make it?

D: If there's free food he'll be here.

APRIL: (*To Czar*) You should show these guys the place.

CZAR: (*To Hoody and D*) You guys wanna take a little tour?

HOODY: Yeah - I want to see where Yummy's bitches spackled.

CZAR: All right. Bri-Bri let's do this. (*To Hoody and D*) C'mon guys.

(*Czar, Hoody and D exit into the house. April and Barb put out more appetizers while Spence makes drinks.*)

SPENCE: I'm sorry but we don't get this in Schaumburg.

BARB: Get what.

SPENCE: This. It's cool. It's exciting.

BARB: It's a bar-be-que Spence.

SPENCE: I know... and I don't want to sound like the stereotypical white guy... even though I sort of am one at this point... but you guys actually have black friends and we - don't. Is that completely racist?

APRIL: Not completely.

SPENCE: So is it less racist to pretend we do this every Saturday? Because the last black guy we had in our house installed cable.

BARB: So it's better to live with people you have absolutely nothing in common with.

SPENCE: I don't know -- these guys seem to be doing okay with it.

(Just then Hoody, D and Czar and the baby re-enter the yard from the house.)

HOODY: See now in the old building -- my auntie's place was like one of y'all's walk-in closets. Her whole thing was like your tub.

CZAR: Yeah it's a lot of house.

HOODY: A lot of house is when your kids have they own room. Y'all got a room to take off shoes.

SPENCE: How long did your aunt live here?

HOODY: Thirty years.

SPENCE: She sell early or she hold out?

HOODY: She didn't sell anything. Just packed her bags. Landlord sold the whole place out from under her.

APRIL: Czar. I need to. *(She gestures, he hands her the baby).* Sorry guys it's dinner time.

(April goes into the house with the baby. Esto enters Hoody's yard and hops the fence into Czar's yard.)

ESTO: Sup, y'all.

95

THE GROUP
  CZAR: C'mon on in -- we're all -- grab a drink --
  SPENCE: Hey -- look who's here --
  HOODY: 'bout time -- I know you ain't been workin'.
  BARB: This is fun -- like a block party --
  D: You were supposed to bring a dessert --

(*Czar hands Esto a beer.*)

ESTO: (*To Spence*) How's Curtis doing man?

SPENCE: Better than Czar.

CZAR: At this point I'm thinking of joining you at Mario Tricocci. How's it going by the way?

(*D glances to Hoody.*)

D: It's -- I love it.

BARB: I love it there too -- I go to Daniel --

D: Daniel crazy --

BARB: Everyone there is so funky -- you just want to like drink espresso and smoke French cigarettes when you're there.

HOODY: D gonna run that place someday --

BARB: I'll do it with you -- you can be the creative one and I'll do the books.

D: Is that what you do?

BARB: It's what I did. I used to work at a big company that -- I left when we had Tyler.

D: You like being home with him?

BARB: I do -- it's -- amazing and consuming... and completely off the radar to the rest of the world, but --

SPENCE: Barb used to manage eight people.

BARB: It's not important.

D: Eight people sounds important.

BARB: It was nine.

SPENCE: She had a high-speed job.

BARB: Way more boring than being a stylist.

D: What did you do?

BARB: I was VP of Brand Awareness and Likeability for Johnson and Johnson's Gauze and Swab division.

ESTO: The fuck is that?

BARB: I was in charge of all personal health absorption products outside of cotton balls for North America.

D: You mean like Q-tips.

BARB: No, not like Q-Tips. Not at all like Q-Tips. They were our biggest competitor. We make two-headed portable cotton swabs.

D: They look like Q-Tips though, right?

BARB: Well... to the untrained eye they might, but our swab heads are actually 18% thicker because of a patented triple fiber technology we developed in the mid-90s. In testing we found it makes for a superior swab of anything from earwax to pus.

HOODY: Okay -- y'all wanna like... listen to some music or something?

(*April enters. She no longer has the baby.*)

APRIL: That's a great idea -- baby's belly is full and he's down. It's time for some music.

SPENCE: And I'm pouring drinks.

HOODY: That's cool, too.

APRIL: Okay, who all wants a cocktail?

CZAR: We got tequila - who's in?

(*Everyone responds positively.*)

CZAR: Okay, here you go, that's for you Hoody, Spence, Esto just hand this one over to D and alright, everybody got one?

APRIL: (*Waving off the tequila and showing her water glass.*) I'm not quite ready for -- yeah --

CZAR: Okay a toast. To - Batman.

(*There is a brief murmur of confusion over the toast, then they all raise their glasses.*)

HOODY: To Cat Woman.

(*They all raise their glasses again.*)

ESTO: To Red Fuckin' Lobster.

(*They all do the shot. The lights go down. When they come back up, the music picks up and they begin to dance. The intensity picks up until everyone is mixing it up and relating to each other on the dance floor. Hoody, D, Esto and Marz form a circle around Spence. They get a kick out his enthusiasm for the moment. From there, the group ends up forming an old-school soul train line where each character performs a character-defining dance move as they come down the line. Then BOOM!*)

We hear what sounds like one of windows in Czar's house shattering and the alarm go off. Everyone screams and stops dancing. Czar runs into the house. April follows. A beat later the alarm stops and we hear a baby crying from inside. Czar emerges from the house holding a cinder block that has been spray painted with gang symbols. April follows holding their child. Czar walks to the fence with the cinder block.)

CZAR: (*To April*) Came right through the window above the bed - landed right on the -

APRIL: Czar just --

CZAR: Glass everywhere --

(*April comes to him. Hoody takes the cinder block out of his hands and calms him down.*)

HOODY: All right man -- this just --

CZAR: Now they're throwing bricks through our windows. (*Yelling out to the neighborhood*) That's enough already, Okay!? That's... enough!

HOODY: You gotta just -- calm down all right? This ain't nothing but --

ESTO: Just a couple shorties showboatin' for they cousins.

HOODY: You ain't dippin' again.

ESTO: I ain't got nothing to do with this. I seen Truth and Future Man hangin' round lately.

HOODY: Truth's in County.

ESTO: Paroled. Good behavior - you believe that?

HOODY: Usually don't come this far West.

(*D looks down the street.*)

D: I don't see nobody out there now.

APRIL: (*To D*) Who are you talking about?

D: Gangbangers.

SPENCE: What do they want?

ESTO: They marking blocks. Tagging space that's all.

HOODY: Happens every year.

CZAR: Yeah well that's great but it's clear they don't like us being here.

ESTO: You'll know if they really don't want you here.

HOODY: They just flexing they muscles that's all. This just noise man.

CZAR: Yeah well -- either way -- (*To the assembled group, Esto in particular*) thanks for coming guys... (*A beat, then more pointedly at Esto*) No really, thanks for coming.

(*People start to shuffle off.*)

SPENCE: You want us to stay?

CZAR: No it's fine -- you guys should go home. I don't know what this is - I don't want you to be in the middle of - whatever this is - It's fine, we're -- thanks guys.

SPENCE: Call me if you need -- cell's on all night.

(*Czar nods. Everyone shuffles out leaving April, Czar, Hoody, and D staring at the cinder block.*)

HOODY: (*To Czar*) You cool, man?

(*A beat.*)

CZAR: Can you help?

HOODY: I could if this was my hood. These kids wasn't even born when I was comin' up... I'm just the old dude at Jiffy Lube. Besides they too scared to listen to anybody right now.

CZAR: They're scared.

(*Hoody nods.*)

CZAR (CONT'D): Of what?

(*A beat. Hoody looks up at the house then back to Czar.*)

CZAR (CONT'D): (*To April*) I need to get something for that window.

APRIL: Czar --

CZAR: I'll be back from Home Depot in an hour. I'm not leaving it like this overnight.

HOODY: I'll watch the place.

APRIL: I can do it - Courtney you don't have to --

CZAR: You're not staying here tonight - (*Gesturing*) not with the baby.

APRIL: Czar. I'm fine. Where am I gonna --

CZAR: Your folks.

APRIL: Czar --

CZAR: Just for tonight. Then you come back home.

D: C'mon. I can drive you out there.

CZAR: That would be great -- I'll bring our car seat out to your car -- (*to April*) you can ride in back in case he gets fussy.

APRIL: D, I can't ask you to do that.

D: You didn't. I offered. C'mon -- just think of it as two women not watching Oprah together.

(*D and April begin to exit.*)

APRIL: Hold on.

(*April stops and grabs the quilt she has been making -- we see that the swatch D gave her is sewn right in the middle of it. She wraps it around the child as she and D leave. Czar follows, pauses, looks over to Hoody and gestures like, "you cool?" Hoody nods then Czar exits. There is a beat as Hoody picks up the cinder block and looks it over alone in the yard. We begin to hear the distance sound of a police siren approaching. The siren gets closer and closer, louder and louder until we simultaneously cut the lights and the siren, leaving the stage silent and black. The last image we see is Hoody alone in the yard with the cinder block.*)

ACT II / SCENE 7: BEING SEEN

(In the darkness we hear a voice.)

CZAR: *(From the darkness)* Invisible is impossible.

(A light comes up on the person speaking. We see it is Czar in a black hooded sweatshirt. He is lit by Esto pointing a handheld flood light at him.)

CZAR (CONT'D): It's a lie. There's no such thing. Everything you do... everything you are and everything you're not... is seen. It is judged and evaluated -- watched and witnessed -- interlocked and interconnected with everything around you and no matter how hard you try... you can never disappear. Fear finds its way through the cracks in your foundation and the holes in your dead bolts... it moves past your rusty latches and over your broken fences until it invades your home -- uninvited, and unflinching, and unapologetic. So you build your walls and you make your calls and you fortify and you camouflage... and you dig in... and you own that fear, and you swallow it, and it feeds you and nourishes you... and crystallizes -- for the first time in your life -- that your only job is to protect your family. Even from your community. And you make peace with the acceptable losses... and make promises that it won't always be this way... and you take comfort in the security of a four digit pass code of your baby's birthday. And you're left with a home... but without a place.

(Esto turns off the flood light and we fade to black.)

103

ACT II / SCENE 8: SHADES OF BLACK AND GREY

(*Lights up on Hoody sitting in his chair in his yard. He has a bandage on his forearm. Czar and April come out of their house into their yard. Czar is holding a stack of papers.*)

CZAR: (*To Hoody*) We just got off the phone with the lawyer -- he's going to call us back --

APRIL: The court date's still (*She gestures*) --

CZAR: He's really good --

APRIL: They're so slow down there -- you can't get an answer without --

CZAR: He's all over this. He's calling us back –

APRIL: At least we have the -- Czar give him -- it's all here --

CZAR: Bail bond is the pink one. You should hang on to that.

(*Czar hands Hoody the pink papers. Esto enters.*)

ESTO: No, no, no -- we don't need nothin' from them man.

CZAR: You're gonna need a lawyer --

ESTO: We don't need your help. Y'all fuckin' done enough already.

HOODY: Yo man --

ESTO: Naw Hoody -- what the fuck -- this a neighborhood thing. These motherfuckers ain't got nothin' to do with it -

CZAR: (*Referencing a form*) Whenever you call they're gonna want the number on the top --

ESTO: You done man -- walk away --

104

HOODY: They trying to help --

ESTO: They ain't helpin' nothin' Hoody -- you know that --

HOODY: Don't tell me what I know man --

ESTO: Somebody's got to talk some sense to you --

CZAR: Look we didn't mean to --

ESTO: I don't give a fuck what you mean to do -- it's what you did. *(To Hoody)* You even tell them 'bout gettin' fired from fuckin' Jiffy Lube? All because y'all come in here and -- and now you want to help.

CZAR: We just want to --

ESTO: Why!

APRIL: Because we live here.

ESTO: Yeah well maybe you shouldn't.

APRIL: Maybe that's not your decision.

ESTO: You don't belong here. This ain't your home. This ain't your hood.

HOODY: Yo man chill your shit --

ESTO: Whatever Hoody -- far's I'm concerned *(big gesture toward April and Czar)* y'all can get the fuck out my hood -- *(gesturing to Czar)* this mutherfucker don't even wanna be here -- just 'cause he got to deal with *(gestures to April)* your bullshit don't mean I have to -- fuck that -- I ain't nobody's bitch!

APRIL: Actually you're everybody's bitch!

CZAR: April --

105

APRIL: You live with your mom, got fired from Red Lobsters -- you can't even figure out how to sell drugs in Garfield Park -- and you steal dishes! And by the way -- you're white! I used to be afraid -- my whole life -- I was taught to be afraid... but right now you're more pathetic than scary -- and I'm more tired than scared -- and I need to go make a bottle for my son.

(April exits into the house.)

ESTO: *(To Czar)* Yo man you need to control that shit --

HOODY: Go.

(Esto goes. There is a beat.)

CZAR: This whole thing is -- I asked you to be there. They got it completely wrong.

HOODY: Tried to tell them that.

CZAR: And?

HOODY: They're cops.

CZAR: Who called them?

HOODY: On patrol -- heard some noise -- saw a black dude holding a cinder block and a broken window on a really nice home. Cuffs was out man.

CZAR: They can't just do that.

HOODY: The fuck they can't.

(A beat.)

CZAR: *(Gesturing to the bandage on Hoody's arm.)* What happened to your --

106

(*A beat.*)

CZAR (CONT'D): They do that?

(*A bea*t.)

HOODY: Hopped the fence to get the fuck back in my own yard. Then they -- (*Hoody gestures.*)

CZAR: They went into your yard.

HOODY: Shit got rough so --

CZAR: Who did? They did?

HOODY: I did.

CZAR: Why would you --

HOODY: Because fuck them! That's why! This my house! Cuffed me in my own motherfucking yard like a goddamn punk! Walked me down the street in front of the whole hood. Didn't even recognize half of 'em. Looked through me like I wasn't even there.

CZAR: I didn't -- this isn't what I --

HOODY: Yeah, well -- ain't really about you anymore is it?

(*We hear the baby cry offstage. April steps out of the house with the baby, waiting for Czar.*)

CZAR: No. It's not.

(*Czar takes a beat then exits into his home.*)

(*We hear the sound of the tumbler on a dead bolt lock and the beeps of a key punch pad from an alarm being set. Hoody reaches into his bag and pulls out the large yellow envelope*

Marz gave him. D enters wearing her cleaning uniform. She stands upstage and watches Hoody. He opens the envelope, reaches in, and pulls out the contract. He takes a beat, notices something, reaches back into the envelope and pulls out a small Starbucks bag. Inside is a small swatch of cloth. He holds it up for D to see. There is a beat.)

End of Play.

NOTES

NOTES

Made in the USA
Columbia, SC
13 November 2017